ROCKY AN

RATMAN

ROCKY AND THE RATMAN

Sylvia Sherry

JONATHAN CAPE
THIRTY-TWO BEDFORD SQUARE
LONDON

For Valerie Kettley

First published 1988
Copyright © 1988 by Sylvia Sherry
Jonathan Cape Ltd, 32 Bedford Square, London WC1B 3EL

British Library Cataloguing in Publication Data:
Sherry, Sylvia
Rocky and the ratman.
I. Title
823′ .914[J]   PZ7
ISBN 0–224–02568–6

Typeset by Falcon Graphic Art Ltd
Wallington, Surrey
Printed in Great Britain by
Alden Press Ltd, Osney Mead, Oxford

CHAPTER

1

"Got the time, mister?"

The old man on the park bench, wearing an old raincoat, a black woolly scarf wrapped round and round his neck and a black woolly cap pulled down to his eyebrows, looked up at Rocky O'Rourke from the sandwich he was eating and then shrank back.

"Haven't gorra watch."

"Well, yer'd think yer'd have a watch," said Rocky, disgusted.

"Lost it."

The old man shoved the remains of his sandwich into a plastic bag and started off through the park. Rocky watched him, wondering, until the reason for this sudden departure dawned on him and he shouted,

"Hi, mister! S'all right! Wasn't goin' ter mug yer for yer watch! Have yer got the —"

But the old man didn't stop – in fact he accelerated.

"Yer wouldn't believe it," muttered Rocky, hunched in his anorak and glaring out over what remained of Princes Park lake which had, for some reason – maybe a leak – reduced itself to a rather large puddle, revealing its bricked-up sides and mucky bottom, one shipwrecked supermarket trolley, an assortment of empty cans and soggy newspapers and two discarded car tyres. A cold wind was churning up muddy ripples, and the ducks were swimming round madly as if trying to keep warm, occasionally turning upside-down to see if there was any food underwater. Rocky's stepsister, Suzie Flanagan, nearly blue with cold, was watching them, fascinated.

There was nothing else happening in the park except for one fisherman sitting optimistically on an upturned wooden box with his line out and two tiddlers doing a decorating job on the dilapidated shelter with knives and spray-paint. Apart from that the place was deserted.

I've seen more going on in a bone-yard, Rocky thought, and it *had* been a wasted Saturday, with all the rest of his gang – the Cats – involved in something and his mother gone off somewhere, leaving him to look after Suzie.

"S'not on," he grumbled to himself. "She should of give us a key. When's she goin' ter get back? I'm not hanging about much longer." And he began to consider getting rid of Suzie to Ellen-from-upstairs and then getting into something interesting himself.

Suzie tugged at the sleeve of his anorak. "Cold, Rocky," she said, shivering. "Cold."

"Yer not de only one. An' it's not *my* fault – it's me mam's. She shouldn't of — what yer doin', yer rubbish? Course yer cold!"

Suzie was standing with her feet in the water.

"Swimmin'."

"Yer not swimmin', but."

"Duck," said Suzie enthusiastically, and paddling with her feet and flapping with her hands she prepared to launch herself into the lake.

Rocky grabbed her just in time, but the two tidd-lers, who had been watching this event, laughed and shouted, "She's a nutter! Throw her in!"

Rocky turned on them, his eyes fierce as a tiger's, his red hair bristling. Suzie was only seven and a strange, silent girl, but she was devoted to Rocky and would follow him anywhere, and nobody was going to put anything over on her while *he* was around.

"I'll do you two!" he shouted. "I'll do youse if youse isn't out of the gates in two minutes!"

It terrified the tiddlers. They shot off with their knives and spray-paint. But that didn't help Rocky. Scaring off a couple of tiddlers was nothing. Problem was what to do next.

"Come on, tatty-'ead," he said, and started towards Princes Boulevard with Suzie racing after him, her shoes squelching and the tattered bow of ribbon in her hair bobbing behind her.

"Cold, Rocky!" she shouted. "Cold!"

"Course yer cold wid yer wet webs! Dis'll warm yer up, but! An' I'll tell yer somethin' – I'll lern yer ter swim!"

As they waited, perilously, in the middle of Princes Boulevard with the Saturday afternoon traffic zipping past in front of and behind them like something out of *Star Wars*, Rocky looked across at the house on the corner with Crown Street next to the empty and vandalised Princes Gate Hotel, which still had its notice board up saying, "Residential – Bed and Breakfast". It was a house that had interested him for some time because it seemed to be empty, and the bushes in the front garden had grown into a small jungle, hiding its windows, but it hadn't been vandalised like the Princes Gate Hotel. Maybe that was because of the rumour that it was haunted by the ghost of a man who'd either been murdered or committed suicide – nobody was certain about this. But it wasn't the ghost that had put Rocky off doing the place – he didn't really believe in them. Aliens, he thought, might exist, but not ghosts. No, what had put him off was the fact that the house was on the corner with Crown Street and was therefore in the Crown Street Gang's territory, and the Crown Street Gang and their leader Murky Evans were fierce and ruthless – worse even than the Cats Gang's sworn enemies, Chick's Lot. So he'd put off investigating. But now he made his mind up, and seeing a gap in the traffic, he grabbed Suzie's hand and shouted, "Come on, tatty-'ead! We're goin' ter suss a place!"

He walked past the house first, pretending he wasn't interested, but really looking out for policemen, then he turned back:

"This is der place, Suzie. I'm sussin' this. Can yer keep dowse like Billy does?"

Suzie looked at him blankly.

"Yer know what I mean? Yer keep on lookin' up an' down der street an' if yer see a scuffer yer yell."

Suzie started yelling straight away – probably just practising.

"Will yer belt up! Yer don't yell till yer see a scuffer – got it?"

Suzie nodded enthusiastically. The house had two tall windows looking onto Princes Boulevard, both covered with dirt and spiders' webs so that you couldn't see through them. After thinking a moment about ghosts and dead men, Rocky got his courage together and cleared a patch of one window with his sleeve and peered in, cupping his hands round his face and pressing against the glass.

He could just make out some big, black furniture, pictures in tarnished gilt frames and pieces of china and glass and silver. Was all right, he thought. If he could get in, there were small things he could pick up. Through the other window he could only see a big golden statue sitting cross-legged and staring at him with still, emerald eyes. Couldn't move that, he decided. Couldn't unload it, anyway. But the other things. . .

He went round the corner of the house into Crown Street where the front door of the house was, with a narrow window of coloured glass on either side. The front door was locked. A high wall went from the end of the house and down to the alley behind, enclosing the back yard, he thought, and there was another door in the alley, but that was locked as well, and there were pieces of glass cemented all along the top of the wall.

Rocky considered the matter. *If* he could find a way of getting in and *if* he could find somebody to buy the loot, it was worth doing. And it would show his brother Joey *and* Nabber Neville that he *could* organise a real robbery. But some things bothered him. If nobody lived there, why had the loot been left and why hadn't the place been done already? Why hadn't the Crown Street Gang or Chick's Lot done it? They were usually as up-to-date as a telephone directory, were Chick and Spadge, when it came to knowing where some loot was. Queer as a nine-pound note, he concluded. It was going to need a lot more sussing and planning, and he went back to get Suzie.

But she wasn't there. She wasn't on the pavement or in the garden, which was shadowy now under the light from the street lamps. He shouted for her, but she didn't appear, and he began to get worried. He hadn't left her for long, but you could never tell with Suzie. If she got frightened or upset, she would take off and find a place to hide in – anywhere she could feel safe – the graveyard behind the Cathedral, an old hut – anywhere.

Among the hurrying pedestrians on the pavement, the only suggestion of a permanent inhabitant was a small boy, would be about ten, thin and pale as a cave insect, with a triangular face like a boggart, who was staring at him.

"Hi!" Rocky shouted. "You wid der head! Yer seen me sister round here – a tiddler?"

The boy said nothing.

"Got plugs in yer ears?"

"What's it worth, but?" asked the boy.

"Worth not gettin' yer head banged!"

The boy seemed to be considering this, then he said, "You Rocky O'Rourke?"

"What if I am?"

"She went in there," and he pointed to the Princes Gate Hotel.

"Right – and clear off – make yer name Walker, wack!"

The sheet of corrugated iron that had been nailed up over the door of the hotel had been pulled away on one side by somebody, and Rocky managed to squeeze through. Inside, it was very dark and smelled of mushrooms – and other things.

"Suzie," he said. There was no reply. He made out a staircase that was hanging off from the wall and a room on one side with no door. He went cautiously into it, his feet crunching on rubble. It looked as if part of the ceiling had fallen in. Nothing moved.

"Suzie!" he shouted. "Yer there, Suzie?"

There was a scuffling noise, and he shouted again. The scuffling came from a corner where there was a tea chest on its side. Rats' nest, he thought, but then he saw a pale face looking out at him from the tea chest.

"What yer doin', yer rubbish?" he shouted, angry but relieved. "What yer think yer are? Dog in a kennel? Told yer to keep dowse!"

"Devil!" Suzie retorted fiercely. "Devil!"

"Get yerself out of that."

"Devil!"

"Der's no devils – but der'll be bugs in der!"

11

Suzie thought about that. "Bugs?" she asked.

"Yes, bugs. Dey bite!"

Suzie scrambled out on all fours, but as Rocky dragged her out of the place she was still muttering, "Devils", in a way that made your flesh creep, and as they went past the empty house she pointed at it and shouted, "Devil!"

"Will yer shurrup! Yer'll start an incident!" And he pulled her round the corner into Crown Street, thinking she must have seen the statue through the window. "What'd he look like – the devil?"

Suzie stopped dead, deep in thought, and then she said, "Black an' white an' up der," and she stretched her hand up as far as she could.

Couldn't beat her for imagination, Rocky thought, and began planning how he would spend the money that he got from the loot in that house. A BMX bike was a definite, and a whole new outfit – trainers and track suit. Also soccer kit. And his mam could have – well, whatever she wanted, even some money for the housey. And Suzie – "Listen, tatty-'ead," he said. "If yer had a lot of money, what would yer buy yerself?"

Suzie didn't have to consider that. "Monster Munchies an' Beastly Wobblies an' Fizzy Cakes," she said.

"No, yer rubbish. I mean a *lot* of money!"

Suzie was up to that as well. "Fish an' two lots of chips an' mushy peas an' a orange."

"Listen, Suzie, yer could have – well, yer could have new jeans an' a anorak an' trainers, an' a new dress – all dat sort of thing."

12

Suzie was obviously astounded. She stopped and looked at him. "Christmas party," she suggested.

"Dat's easy! Come on!" and he started running, reflecting that he'd have to try to join the Baptist Youth Club again, if they would have him, so that he could get tickets for their Christmas party – if they had one. He'd been done out of it twice!

"Doin' a marathon, are yer? Or have yer just given up old friends?" an angry voice asked.

Rocky stopped. It was Mr Oliver, who *was* a friend, standing outside Mrs Abercrombie's house, which had been turned into flats and where he was caretaker. And Rocky immediately felt guilty.

"'Lo, Mr Oliver," he said, in a conciliatory way. "How's it?"

"How's it? What yer mean, how's it? What happened ter you lot this morning? I was early in Prinney Park for the match, and if you and the Cats' team and their opponents turned up, I saw nothin' of them!"

"Sorry, Mr Oliver. Forgot ter tell yer there wasn't a match this mornin'. All der Cats was doin' somethin' – like havin' ter see their aunts and uncles, and Little Chan was playin' his flute at the Chinese Centre and the Nabber's dad's got some videos."

"Not very professional, is it? Being that casual? *You* should be takin' more notice as captain. After all, I'm givin' up time ter coach and referee – *and* yer lucky ter have me!"

That was true and Rocky knew it. Mr Oliver had played for Liverpool at one time – been a star player until he'd lost an arm in a car accident and become a wingy.

"Won't happen again. I'll have a word with Billy about next Saturday – an' after all I *did* get yer the job as caretaker here – dat's somethin' after all."

"Yer right there," Mr Oliver conceded. "That *is* somethin'. But *you* get next Saturday organised and keep me informed. And why's Suzie shiverin' like that? And mud up to her ankles! Where've yer had her?"

"We was in Prinney Park and she went paddlin' in der lake."

Suzie smiled, happy at being taken notice of. "Wet webs," she said, triumphantly. "Got wet webs."

"Get her home and get her webs dry den, Rocky," said the wingy. "Is yer mam in?"

Rocky shrugged. "Don't know. She wasn't. That's why we was in the Park."

"Well, your Joey's in. Saw his bike outside when I come from the pub. But just in case," he added, knowing Rocky's mother's habit of departing on her own business and leaving Rocky and Suzie locked out, "shake."

Rocky put his hand out happily, because he knew what to expect when the wingy shook hands, and he felt the coins in his palm. Would be maybe forty pence, he thought.

"Thanks, Mr Oliver. See yer. Come on, tatty-'ead!" And as they ran through the darkening Square to Number 3, he added, "Could get some chips ternight!"

CHAPTER

2

St Catherine's Square, where Rocky lived, was lit by two street lamps, one at the far end where the archway leading to St Catherine's Buildings was, and the other diagonally opposite where the Steps were that led down to Larkspur Lane. They illuminated the patch of trodden ground in the middle of the Square that had once been a garden and where there was an abandoned car and a builder's hut, which had also been abandoned and was slowly disintegrating along with the car. The tiddlers from Joseph Terrace had helped both processes by removing parts of each at intervals, when they had need of them. The light from the street lamps sparkled on the broken milk bottles and discarded take-away trays from Chan's Chippy and the chrome on Joey O'Rourke's bike, which was parked outside Number 3. And on the pavement, Ellen-from-upstairs's baby was sitting in his pram, looking pink-nosed even in the lamplight.

"Yer all right, Trevor?" asked Rocky, pausing to give the pram a friendly shake up and down, and in return the baby gave him a sneeze. Catching his death, Rocky thought, and looked up at Ellen's window, where there was a light on.

"Hi, Ellen!" he shouted.

After a few moments, Ellen pushed the window open and leaned out, her long blonde hair golden in the lamplight:

"Who's it?"

"S'me. He's gettin' pneumonia down here."

"Oh. Right. I'll fetch him." And the window was shut.

Funny, Rocky thought. Ellen was usually more inclined to have a talk. She seemed a bit up-tight. And Suzie was glaring at Joey's bike and muttering "Bad!"

"He's not bad, our Joey. Just evil. Come on, Suzie."

They went into the passage of Number 3 with its tattered linoleum and dim light bulb and then into the first of the two rooms Rocky's family had. The electric fire was going full blast and Joey O'Rourke was lying back in one of the chairs beside it, his feet on the stool, a cigarette in his hand and his face in the sports pages of the *Liverpool Echo*. He jerked round as they came in, and Suzie got behind Rocky.

"'Lo, skin. How's things?" asked Joey, genial as Santa Claus in the Grotto at Lewis's.

"Dey was great before you come back!"

Rocky dropped on to the sofa behind the table and Suzie got behind the sofa, for protection.

"Yer always was a good skin!" And Joey grinned to himself, turning back to his paper.

Rocky wondered why Joey was so cheerful. He must be into something.

"Wur's me mam?" he asked.

"Haven't seen her. Not been in long, but."

16

There was something smug and confident about Joey that made Rocky angry. *And* he had a key to their flat and could get in when he liked, and him and Suzie hadn't. Wasn't right. After all, Joey was a no-good and a coward, and just came or cleared off when he felt like it. Wasn't bothered about him and Suzie.

Rocky considered things, and then asked, casually, "Inter somethin', like?"

"Tell yer sometime – when it's all set up. Is interestin'."

Which only made Rocky more curious.

Suzie whispered from behind the sofa, "Wet webs, Rocky."

"Get yer shoes off den, and put dem in front of the fire."

There was a pause, then Suzie whispered, not wanting to go near Joey, "Don't like *him*."

"He'll not eat yer, but. Get yer slippers on and let's have yer shoes. And what's der ter eat?" Rocky went to investigate. There was a pie and a packet of crisps. Rocky had had enough pies, so he held it up to Joey and asked, "Yer want dis?"

Joey didn't, so Rocky gave some crisps to Suzie and had some himself. And as he crunched he reflected about things. He had to get the Cats together to see what they could do about the loot in that house. That was certain. But he might also be able, at that moment, since there was nothing to eat in the flat except that pie – and nobody knew when his mother would come home – to get something out of Joey, and save the wingy's forty pence.

17

"Hi, Joey," he said, persuasively, "if yer still workin' for der Queen, yer should have some money."

"What about it?"

"Yer could buy us some chips, like. I would go an' get dem," he offered, generously.

Joey sat up. "Great idea, skin. Yer on. Here, get two fish and some chips an' go round ter the off-licence in Joseph Terrace an' get a couple of bottles—"

"Can't, but. Dey won't serve me. Under age."

"Go meself, den."

"Give us der key, but – I'll be back first."

Joey, in his helmet and leathers, revved up and roared away in the direction of Princes Boulevard, and the woman from Number 4 shot out and demanded, "That yer brother makin' all that noise?"

But Rocky couldn't shop Joey, whatever he thought of him. "No, missus," he said, "was one of dem from Joseph Terrace. Come on, tatty-'ead. Told yer we'd get some chips, didn't I?" And he headed for the Steps with Suzie following.

Larkspur Lane was Blackpool illuminations compared to St Catherine's Square. There was the light on in front of the police station, and the neon shining behind the wire frames over Pa Richardson's grocery, and the newsagent's window already sparkling with a few strands of tinsel in anticipation of Christmas, with a notice saying, "Join our Christmas Club". Chan's chippy was like a theatrical set in which Mrs Chan stood alternately swirling chips round in one of the pans and piling fried fish into the heated cabinet, while her eldest daughter carefully wrapped up orders, diminishing the queue at the counter. The only dark spot in the lane was the mysterious shop with its window full of sun-faded baby clothes and blankets and dead flies, with a notice saying, "Under new manijment" – though the new management didn't seem to have turned up.

Mrs Chan looked round as Rocky and Suzie came into the warm, fishy-smelling shop and joined the queue. She did that with every new customer, but when she saw Rocky her eyes became watchful. Rocky didn't have a very good reputation with Mrs Chan.

The slow-moving queue made Rocky restive and his mind started going over things, and he got an idea for some forward-planning.

"Keep der place, Suzie," he said. "Have ter see if Little Chan's in," and he went to the other end of the counter where the till was and the door that led into the Chans' living room behind the shop.

He leaned over the counter and shouted through the open door, "Hi – Chan!"

Little Chan appeared. "What's it, Rocky?" he asked, anxiously, not knowing what to expect.

"How'd the playin' go?" Rocky asked – this was for Mrs Chan's benefit.

"Was all right."

"Well, listen." Rocky dropped his voice, confidentially. "I've got a job sussed out, and I want all the Cats in the hideout termorrer."

Little Chan looked even more anxious. "But, Rocky, it is not good to do places. . ."

19

"Could talk about it, but," Rocky suggested, persuasively. "Can yer phone Billy?"

"I cannot just use the phone."

"Only take a second. Tell him ter phone de Nabber an' tell de Nabber ter phone Beady, right? Hideout, termorrow, three o'clock."

Little Chan knew that his mother was watching them, but he knew also that she was too busy just then to do any questioning, and his father was out, so he said, "I will try, Rocky," and went back into the room behind the shop. He thought it over for a few minutes and then took a risk and phoned Billy Griffiths, hoping he wouldn't get Billy's mother or father. But it was Billy who answered, and he gave the message.

"Tomorrow, hideout, three – all right," Billy said. "What's it for?"

"Rocky has got a plan. He will tell us. Can you let the Nabber know, and ask him to tell Beady?"

"Don't think the Nabber'll answer with the videos goin', but I'll ask him."

The plastic bag was heavy and warm and odorous of fish and chips, and Rocky started towards the Steps, confident that he was getting things moving about that house and looking forward to the food.

"Come on, Suzie," he shouted. "Beat yer ter the Steps!"

At the bottom of the Steps he paused, warily, because the Steps weren't well-lit and he'd been attacked by a terrorist on them once. In any case,

20

you could be mugged for your fish and chips, if you weren't careful. But the Steps were empty.

"Right, Suzie," he said. "Get yer skates on or dis lot'll be cold."

But as they got to the top of the Steps a tall figure barred their way, a man with white hair, wearing a long black overcoat, his arms outstretched, and he began talking:

"There's eight and ate, and tart and tart, and lies and lies, and flies and flies. . ."

"Devil!" shrieked Suzie.

Rocky grabbed her hand. "Dat'll do *you*, mister! Geroff, or I'll pin one on yer!" he shouted, and dragged Suzie past the man and across the Square to Number 3. Then he looked back. The man was still there, staring at them.

"Clear off, or I'll have der scuffers to yer!" Rocky shouted.

"There's try and fail!" shouted the man.

He's a nutter, Rocky thought. Suzie's hand was clutching his, and she was muttering, "Devil, devil, devil. . ."

"S'all right, tatty-'ead. S'all right." And he pulled her into the house, thankful that he'd conned Joey into handing over the key, and opened the door of the flat.

His mother was standing in the middle of the room, looking distracted.

"What's goin' on here?" she demanded. "What's the telly an' the fire left on for – and the light? Who's goin' ter pay the bills? An' wur've *you* been? And what's up wid *her*?" (Suzie was scowling at her and chuntering fiercely.) "And how did yer get in, anyway?"

"An' wur've *you* been? We've been shiverin' in Prinney Park all de afternoon. Wur was *you*? Leave us widout a key, yer do! An' Suzie's been frightened by a nutter on de Steps – an' *you* don't care, an' I'll tell that feller Flanagan that yer married—"

"Yer'll what? You threatenin' me – yer mother?" Mrs Flanagan was outraged.

"Yes," retorted Rocky. "Dat's what I'm doin'."

"The nurve! I'll batter yer for that!"

"It's Joey, in't it? But yer'll not batter him, will yer?"

"Joey? What yer mean, Joey?"

"Back, in't he? Give us der money for fish an' chips, an' give us a key, 'cos *he's* got one, an' he was goin' ter the off-licence, an' *he* left everythin' on, see? But yer won't blame *him*, will yer? Yer won't batter *him*?"

Mrs Flanagan suddenly softened and glowed. "Joey's back? That's luvely! An' what a good lad buyin' us the supper! How long's he stoppin'? Here, I'll put the fish an' chips in the oven till he gets back, and we'll all celebrate. An' what's more," she added, "if yer have ter know, I've been ter yer Auntie Chrissie's, because she's not well. And *that's* none of Flanagan's business. He's never here, anyway!"

Rocky sat down on the sofa and picked up one of his comics, and Suzie sat down beside him, since Joey wasn't there, and watched her stepmother warily.

"What's der ter celebrate?" asked Rocky. "An' I'm not waitin' for our Joey. Yer never know wid

22

him. He could come home wid der church bells termorrer."

"That's enough of yer lip! And why's there just three fish?"

"That's Joey, see. He's economical," said Rocky, pleasantly. "In fact, he told me ter only get two, but it's as well I upted it, in't it?"

"We'll share them out. Anyway, what we're celebratin' is there's a card come from Flanagan. He's on his way home. Here." And she took a postcard from behind the clock on the mantelpiece and handed it to Rocky, and then turned away to look at herself in the mirror beside the clock, patting her hair and putting some lipstick on.

Rocky examined the card. On one side there were some Arabs in black clothes riding yellow camels over orange sand, and on the other side Flanagan had written, "On my way. Back soon."

"When's soon, but?" asked Rocky, interested. He hadn't liked Flanagan when his mother married him after his father's death, but he'd been all right, had Flanagan, in the end, until he'd gone off on an oil tanker to make some money.

"Not sure when. But he's comin'." And Mrs Flanagan went to fill the kettle.

"Yer hear that, tatty-'ead?" Rocky said to Suzie. "Yer dad's comin' back."

Suzie stared at him blankly.

"Yer dad – yer know, yer dad?"

But suddenly Suzie clenched both hands and began beating them on the table, yelling, "No dad! No dad!

23

No dad!" over and over again, until Mrs Flanagan shouted, "Will yer stop her!" and Rocky grasped Suzie's wrists and turned her towards him.

"Will yer give it up, Suzie?" he said, earnestly. "Will yer shurrup? An' here – yer can colour in de Alien's head in me comic. Yer can colour him in wid dis red biro, see?"

Suzie looked at him, a bit dazed, then she nodded, took the comic and the biro and began fiercely scribbling red over the Alien's head whenever it appeared.

Mrs Flanagan turned back to the cooker, and Rocky watched Suzie. There was nothin' yer could do with her, he thought. Couldn't understand her. She couldn't have forgotten her dad, could she?

"Are yer deaf?" asked Mrs Flanagan, from the cooker. "Der's somebody at the door."

Rocky went to open it, and Joey came in.

"Hello, luv!" exclaimed Mrs Flanagan. "Yer back! How long yer stayin'?"

"Cold as a nun's bum out there," said Joey, thrusting a brown paper bag at her. "Here's the bevvy, mam. Pour us a glass and let's have the supper. An' I'm stayin' for a bit – got a job on round here."

"That's smashin', Joey! What sort of a job?"

"Can't tell yer. Confidential, yer know, like." And Joey sat down at the table with his glass of beer, superior and triumphant.

"Smashin'!" said Mrs Flanagan, rattling plates. "Everythin's happenin' tergether. Flanagan's on his way back, as well."

24

That upset Joey, as Rocky knew it would. His face collapsed like a ruptured custard. "When's he comin'?" Joey asked.

"Well – not termorrer. Don't know yet. Just said he was on his way."

"Dat's all right then," muttered Joey. "I'll be out of here before den."

Mrs Flanagan didn't hear this. Happily she put out the plates of fish and chips, raised her glass of beer and said, "Ter Joey an' his job."

"Ter Joey," said Rocky, "and the day when he goes."

"That'll do *you*!" Mrs Flanagan exclaimed indignantly. "Don't yer say that sort of thing about yer brother!"

"What've I said? Just hoping he gets de job done!"

Joey leant across the table towards Rocky and said, "Don't you worry, wack! When this job's done I'll be lookin' for a tax haven!"

"That's nice," said Rocky. "It'll be Walton Jail again, will it?"

Mrs Flanagan stood up and said fiercely, "Get that food down yer quick, and get ter bed!"

Rocky lay in bed, a BMX poster showing somebody doing the Cherry Picker stuck on the wall behind him, and read his comic. It wasn't worthwhile getting up, because it was Sunday, and Sunday was generally a write-off. The flat was cold and Mrs Flanagan took hours to surface and anyway there was nothing to do. Sometimes Sunday didn't happen at all.

Suddenly Joey, in the other bed, sat up and said, "But der's de wall – de wall!" And then he subsided.

Got his mind on Walton Jail, Rocky thought, but then there were shouts from the next room, and Rocky leapt out of bed. In the living room, Suzie was standing up on the bed she shared with her stepmother and screaming, and Mrs Flanagan was shaking her.

"Stop batterin' her, mam!" Rocky shouted. "What's she done?"

"This is what she's done!" Mrs Flanagan held up one of her valuable collection of paper-backed romances which Suzie, obviously bored and looking for something to do, had scribbled over with the red biro Rocky had given her. "I'll belt her round the Square for that!"

"What's all dis?" asked Joey, appearing, blear-eyed, in the doorway, and at that moment there was a knocking on the ceiling which shocked them all into silence.

"Who's doin' that?" asked Mrs Flanagan in a hushed voice. "Wouldn't be Ellen. She's never knocked down. She wuddent."

"Be her husband," said Rocky.

"Well, if it is, he'll get the edge of my tongue!" said Mrs Flanagan angrily, and then she shouted, looking up at the ceiling, "Stop that bangin'!"

The result was another banging, and Mrs Flanagan exclaimed, "It's *him*! Has ter be! And he wouldn't be up there if she hadn't married him – and I did their wedding tea! The nurve! Come on, Joey!" And Mrs Flanagan shot out of the room in her dressing-gown and curlers.

Joey hesitated.

26

"Go on den, skin," said Rocky encouragingly.

"Haven't got the time," said Joey. "Got the job to see to."

Rocky went out into the passage. His mother was standing on the stairs, talking to Ellen-from-upstairs, who was leaning over the banister with her blonde hair falling over her face.

"Sorry, Mrs Flanagan," she was saying. "I'm that sorry. But me husband couldn't stand the row, yer know like, 'cos it started Trevor off crying. Yer know what it's like."

Mrs Flanagan calmed down. "I know, luv. Nobody better. Forget about it. But if he starts that knockin' again, I'll have the police in – yer can tell him!"

"All right, Mrs Flanagan. Hello der, Rocky. Yer all right?"

"All right. How's Trevor den?"

Ellen gave a sob and disappeared.

Mrs Flanagan came down the stairs. "I don't like the way things is goin' on up there," she said, and went into the living room and sat down in her chair. Suzie was still standing on the bed, glaring.

Rocky shut the door. "What's der for the breakfast?" he asked.

"Yer'll have ter get what yer can," said his mother. "It's too much for me, havin' this sort of thing this early."

And Rocky, noting that according to the alarm clock on the mantelpiece it was eleven o'clock, started making jam butties.

"Here," he said, handing one to Suzie, who sat down on the bed and began to eat. "Yer want one, mam?"

"Well," Mrs Flanagan conceded, "I'd better have something."

Eating his own butty, Rocky thought about the job he was planning. It would be a bigger job than Joey's – had to be with all that loot. Could be worth a fortune, even just some of the small things, but he had to persuade the Cats to help him, because he couldn't get over that back wall into the yard by himself. He tried to think of ways of doing it. Maybe a rope ladder with hooks on the end. He could stand on the Nabber's shoulders and throw the hooked end so that it hooked on the wall and – but then there was the glass. But he could smash that with a hammer. He would get it thought out. He knew he would.

At three o'clock, Rocky was standing outside Number 3. There was a temporary afternoon silence over the city, broken only by a passing jogger coming from St Catherine's Buildings and crunching across some broken glass as he headed for Princes Park and freedom. Suzie was absorbed in digging holes with an old spoon in the hard clay of the abandoned garden, and planting in them whatever weeds and grasses she could find. There was a good crop of weeds, especially under the abandoned car and round the builder's hut. Over towards the River Mersey, against a flat, grey sky, the square tower of the Anglican Cathedral seemed to be watching her and Rocky and the jogger.

"Yer all right, Suzie?" Rocky asked, but Suzie only grunted. "Well, yer'll be all right till I get back?"

Suzie grunted again, and Rocky leapt on to the low stone wall round the garden and ran along it, and leapt off again when he reached the top of the Steps, because that was where the Cats' hideout was, in the basement of the crumbling vicarage beside the old black church. Rocky had found the hideout by forcing open the door of the basement, and the Cats had furnished it with whatever they could get. Rocky had personally nicked an old carpet put out for the bin men.

The hideout was secret. Well, it had been until the time Chick's Lot had found it, but Rocky had fought and threatened and blackmailed Chick and Spadge so that they wouldn't dare come near the place again. Rocky never went straight into the hideout – he always ran past it first, as though he were going somewhere else, then if nobody was watching he doubled back and shot down the steps into the basement. As he ran past this time, he noticed that Billy Griffith's tricycle was chained to the railings round the basement. Billy was secretary and manager of the Cats' football team, but he'd been crippled by polio and could only get around easily on his tricycle.

Rocky turned back, leapt down the steps to the basement, gave the Cats' secret knock on the door and went inside. "'Lo der, wacks!" he said.

"It's Daddy Christmas," said Nabber Neville.

"I think it is super Rocky," said Little Chan.

"It's a alien from outer space," said Beady Martin.

Billy did not say anything.

29

It put Rocky out, that reception did, because he felt the atmosphere was hostile, and as leader of the gang he did not expect that.

"What's up wid youse?" he demanded angrily. "Somebody been gettin' at youse?"

Nobody answered, and Rocky glared round at them. Then he went to light some candles and the old oil heater which didn't give out a lot of heat but had a nice red glow. He filled the kettle and put it on the heater. It would take ages to boil, but they had plenty of time. He turned back to the gang, who were sitting round the card table. The hideout was damp and dark and the old card table was shaky, and so were the stools, and the sofa was a mess, but it *was* theirs, and it looked quite cheerful now. But there was something wrong with the Cats, and it could only have come from the Nabber, who was the one who was relaxed.

"Right." Rocky sat down on a stool. "What's up wid youse?"

"This plan of yours," said Nabber Neville, chewing something – the Nabber was always chewing something. "Another one. What's it this time? This another empty deri yer plannin' ter do? Like that shop yer had us spending hours gettin' into and der was nothin' there?"

"I've sussed this place," said Rocky angrily. "It's on Prinney Boulevard, and I've looked through the front windows. It's a big place, and it's full of stuff, and it's empty."

"Great!" said the Nabber. "Full of stuff and empty? That's great!"

30

"I'll *do* you, Nabber Neville! Yer *know* what I mean!"

"What sort of stuff?"

"Der's all sorts – der's silver an' gold—"

"Wur yer goin' ter get rid of it to, but?"

"Dat's your side of things, in't it. *You're* de feller wid de contacts!"

That silenced the Nabber as he thought over his contacts in the gold and silver business. Beady, Billy and Little Chan felt relieved because they thought the Nabber had been put in his place, but they were also silent as they thought about what could be involved in this scheme of Rocky's.

"The enthusiasm," Rocky said at last, "is shatterin'. Don't know why I bother wid youse."

"But, Rocky," said Billy, reasonably, "it could be dangerous."

"Course it could. That's de whole point, in't it? Somethin' ter make yer sweat! Oh, come on! Brew up, Beady, and we'll have a cuppa and a game of cards. All youse is good for."

They were all rather subdued as they played cards and drank tea and ate biscuits provided by Beady, who had found a packet lying on the pavement – especially knowing that Rocky's red hair was bristling with annoyance at their lack of enthusiasm, though in fact Rocky was very pleased that he'd put the Nabber in his place.

At last Billy suggested quietly, knowing Rocky was keen about his plan, "We could go an' look at the place."

"Right – termorrer night!" said Rocky.

31

"Tomorrow I cannot go," said Little Chan.

"Yer not playin' that flute again?" asked Rocky.

"It is a concert."

"Right. Tuesday – comin' back from school?"

The Cats agreed. Even the Nabber agreed, but condescendingly.

"Right. Hi – our Joey's back, an' he says he's inter somethin' big."

The Nabber was immediately interested. "What's it?" he asked.

"Confidential." Rocky frowned over his cards.

"He could cut us in," said the Nabber.

"If our Joey was a ghost he wouldn't give yer a fright, he's that mean," said Rocky; and added, "Der wingy's mad wid us not turnin' up on Saturday. Have ter get the team tergether for next Saturday – all right, Billy?"

Billy nodded, concentrating on his cards.

"An' can yer get a fixture? Any team goin'?"

Billy frowned, thinking of two things at once. "Not sure. Not a lot goin' on. Chick's Lot's not tergether yet. Think there's a new team in Anderson Road, and there's the Allsorts in Danby Street. Could try them."

"What's de Allsorts?" asked Beady.

Billy shrugged. "Just the Allsorts. Mixed, yer know, like." And with quiet triumph he laid down his cards. "My game," he said.

"This place we're sussing," said Beady, as they finished the tea and biscuits. "Wurabouts is it on the Boulevard?"

"Corner with Crown Street."

Beady, Billy and Little Chan looked at one another apprehensively. Then Beady said, "That's the Crown Street Gang's territory, but."

Rocky shrugged. "Could be just on de boundary, yer know like. Der'll be no bother from dem."

"Course not. No bother," said the Nabber, casually collecting the cards. That didn't make Beady and Billy and Little Chan feel any better, and it made Rocky definitely suspicious. There was something sarcastic about the Nabber's tone of voice, but he decided to ignore it.

"Day after termorrer den. Dis is a big job, mind."

"Big as you?" asked the Nabber, referring to the fact that Rocky was the smallest of the Cats, except for Little Chan.

"Yes," Rocky retorted, impressively, "it's *that* big!"

But the Nabber wasn't impressed. Casually he stood up, stretched and turned to get something from behind the sofa and put it on his head. It was a ten-gallon cowboy hat.

"Right," he said. "See yer," and moved laconically towards the door.

The Cats were stunned.

"Wur'd he get *that* from?" asked Beady, awed.

"Nicked it out of Lewis's," said Rocky, contemptuous but impressed.

"Would be his dad got it in Texas," said Billy.

"It looks very heavy," said Little Chan.

"Hope it breaks his neck den," said Rocky.

★

It was one of the rules that the Cats left the hideout cautiously and separately. Rocky was the last to leave, sitting by himself for a while and thinking about the Nabber's hat. Why couldn't Flanagan have gone to Texas like the Nabber's father did, instead of going off on an oil tanker? Then he could have brought Rocky an even bigger hat. What could he bring back from the Middle East, except maybe a camel? But then he consoled himself, thinking about that house with its loot. Would be a better job than Joey's. Would be better than a cowboy hat!

He blew out the candles, closed the door of the hideout carefully behind him and ran up the steps into the lights of the Square. Somebody there was shouting, "Let me in! Let me in, yer clock-faced jigger rabbit!"

It was Mr Oliver, and he'd obviously had a few pints! Rocky ran across to Mrs Aber's, where the wingy was hammering at the door with his one fist and shouting.

"What's it, Mr Oliver?" he asked.

Mr Oliver turned and swayed cautiously towards him.

"S'bad, Rocky. S'bad as possible."

"How's dat, Mr Oliver?"

"S'my turn. She's locked me out." He leant heavily on the gate with his one arm.

"Yer mean yer wife?"

"Wasn't happy wid the paintin' I done – and then I went out for a couple of . . ."

"Not gorra key, but?"

"In my jacket pocket. In der house. With her." And suddenly the wingy ran back up the path and started hammering on the door again and shouting.

"Hi, Mr Oliver," Rocky began, but then a voice beside him said,

"What's goin' on?"

It was Constable McMahon, from Larkspur Lane police station.

"Nothin'. S'nothin'," said Rocky quickly, not wanting the wingy to get into trouble.

"Doesn't sound like nothin'. Now then, Dave Oliver, what yer up to? Creatin' a disturbance—"

"So would you, if yer was locked out of yer home – yer *home!*"

"Yer've had too much, haven't yer? Now, I don't want the bother of havin' ter take yer in on a drunk and disorderly, and fill in a lot of forms. Got a lot more important things ter do, like tryin' ter find out who's pushing drugs round here. So give it up, Dave."

"S'all right sayin' give it up," objected Rocky, who had had experience of this kind of situation, "but he's locked out. So what yer doin' about it?"

"Yer wife in?" asked McMahon.

"She's always in – except when she's out," said the wingy, more soberly. "Forget it, Mac. It's domestic."

McMahon hesitated, then he asked, "Sure of that?"

"Yer know I am."

"Right. Leave it with yer," and the constable departed in the direction of Larkspur Lane police station.

There was a moment of silence as Rocky and the wingy considered the situation, then Rocky said, "Yer goin' ter lose yer job again, Mr Oliver, if yer don't watch it, yer know like."

Mr Oliver sighed. "Yer right, Rocky. Yer always is, except when yer not. Some things yer just have ter live with – that's right, in't it?"

"S'right, Mr Oliver. Like me mam."

"That's right. Like yer mam."

There was another moment of silence during which Rocky made up his mind.

"Mr Oliver, yer know that house along from Princes Gate Hotel, the one on the corner with Crown Street?"

It took the wingy's mind off his troubles. "I do," he said, but added suspiciously, "What about it? You up ter somethin' yer shouldn't be?"

"S'not that, Mr Oliver. Not up ter nothin'. Was just thinkin'. Der's nobody livin' there, is there?"

"Thinkin' of movin' in?"

"Thinkin' it could be done by somebody."

Mr Oliver considered the matter. "Yer right. I'll have a word with McMahon about it."

This was the last thing Rocky wanted. "No need, but. Looks all right, yer know like. Locked up."

And to Rocky's relief, the wingy went into a reflective mood. "Tell yer somethin', Rocky. The feller that used ter live in that house – I knew him. Was a 'Pool supporter. Never missed a match. An' I got ter know him well. He was a antique dealer, tradin' from home. Bit of a nutter, and got queerer as he got older. Well, we all do, don't we? Yer must have noticed it in yerself."

36

"What yer mean?" Rocky demanded angrily, but the wingy winked.

"If the cap fits . . . But he *did* get queer. Would drive the wrong way round roundabouts and got nicked for dangerous drivin' because he was goin' too slow. That kind of thing. Then he was on a trip somewhere and the car packed in, and he left it at a garage for repairs and forgot where the garage was. Never got it back. Was a miser as well, mind. Never put his hand in his pocket, and always disappeared when it was his turn to pay for a round of drinks. Lived in his coat and scarf and gloves when the weather was cold, because he didn't believe in payin' for heatin'. Haven't seen him for years – not since Jesus was playin' fullback for Israel. Well," he corrected himself, "don't *think* I've seen him around. Never heard what happened to him. Must be dead. But after all," he added reflectively, "there's a lot of folk yer don't know what happened to, isn't there?"

"That's right, Mr Oliver," Rocky agreed, though he couldn't personally think of any off-hand. But what Mr Oliver said fitted with the loot in that house – antiques, and worth a lot. Was a gold mine. Sooner he got the place done, the better, before the man's relatives or the Crown Street Gang got moving in on it.

CHAPTER

3

It was getting dark, but it wasn't dark enough for the street lights to be on, so you couldn't see things very clearly in the alley behind the houses. The Cats Gang walked quickly and quietly and cautiously, because of the Crown Street Gang. Rocky went first, on the look-out for trouble in front, Billy on his tricycle was sussing the area generally, Beady and Little Chan then followed and the Nabber was supposed to be looking out for trouble behind, but it was Rocky who first heard foot-steps approaching and hissed, "Freeze!" The Cats froze as a bulky, solemn figure in boots and a back-pack came steadily along the alley.

"It's Murky," whispered Beady. "Murky Evans. He's the Crown Street Gang's leader."

"No, it's not," said the Nabber, uninvolved and chewing something. "S'not him." And the man *did* plod on past them without a glance.

The Cats were relieved, but Rocky was suspicious. There was something too laid back about the Nabber, and it couldn't be just on account of the ten-gallon hat which he had been showing off in for two days.

They went on cautiously until Rocky said quietly, "This is it. This is the place." The Cats stopped, but there was nothing to see – only the brick wall with the door in it.

"This the way in?" asked Beady, and tried to open the door, and gave it a shake and a kick, but it didn't open. "Der's a problem here," he said. "If the doors an' windows is locked we'll never get in. And that broken glass along the top – cut yer to ribbons. Never get in. Like Fort Knox."

"Think we should give it up, Rocky," said Billy, frowning down at the handlebars of his tricycle. "Too difficult." He didn't add "too dangerous" but that's what he was thinking, and he would have been pleased if Rocky decided to give it up.

"Yes, and it's getting dark," said Little Chan, thinking he was making an important point.

"Dat's good but," said Rocky. "Means nobody'll see us, an' I can get over der wall – I can put me anorak over the glass!"

The Cats considered the situation. The Nabber considered it as he leant against the wall in the shadow of his hat. The others considered it from the point of view that they didn't want to disappoint Rocky, but they *were* in dangerous territory and they could see no way of getting into the house even if they had wanted to – and they didn't.

And there was a definite feeling of danger in that alley. The sky was still a pale blue with a big white moon in it, but a bank of navy blue clouds was coming in from the Mersey over the Anglican Cathedral, threatening to take over the moon and making the alley shadowy and menacing.

"Could try some other place," suggested Beady.

"Der's *no* other place!" said Rocky, exasperated. "Yer don't *know* dis place – it's got everythin' in it!"

"Maybe," said Little Chan hopefully, "it would be advisable to come back tomorrow."

"Der's no point in that! Where's the point in that?" asked Rocky angrily. "I've sussed this place – I'm tellin' youse – it'll be like takin' a ice-cream off Ellen-from-upstairs's baby!" He took a moment to calm down. "Look," he said, "I'm goin' over der wall. . ."

But at that very moment a man appeared on top of the wall, coming over from the house. He hesitated on top, and then dropped down on to the pavement, groaned a bit and ran off in a stumbling sort of way.

"Told yer," whispered Rocky, as the man disappeared, "told yer there was loot in there. We better get in before it goes. Bunk us up, Nabber."

"Bunk yerself up for a change," retorted the Nabber, who was going off the whole thing. "Yer always the one that has ter be bunked up."

"Because I'm the only one that knows what ter look for, *see*? *You* couldn't recognise a fat man hidin' behind a lamp-post! An' all right! *I'll* bunk Beady up!" Rocky decided democratically, and he bent down while a rather reluctant Beady climbed on to his shoulders. The Nabber leant against the wall, giving the whole thing up.

"It's that hat – it's gone to his head!" said Rocky as he slowly stood up straight, bringing Beady level with the top of the wall and its broken glass.

For a few moments Beady looked over the wall, then he said, "Let's down, Rocky – quick!" When he got down, he looked pale, which was unusual for Beady since he was brown.

"What's it, Beady?" Rocky asked, bewildered.

"Don't know – but it's – it's – don't know."

"Better leave it, Rocky," advised Billy.

"No – I'm havin' a look. Can yer bunk me, Beady?"

Beady rubbed a hand over his face. "Just about," he said. "Then I'm getting away from this place!"

Beady slowly stood up, and Rocky looked over the wall. There was nothing to see, only a dark yard and a dark window on the ground floor of the house and another dark window above it. It was all dark, but as Rocky watched, he gradually made out the figure of a man standing at the ground floor window, quite still and staring out. Rocky had the feeling that the man was staring at him. There was something menacing and creepy about him, and Rocky began to understand how Beady had felt. And, remembering what the wingy had told him about the nutter who had lived there, he was convinced that he was looking at a ghost.

"Let's down, Beady," he whispered, and at the same time the street lamps came on and a voice asked, "What are you lot up to?" It was Constable McMahon.

Billy gripped the handlebars of his tricycle tightly and Little Chan stood tensely beside him, while the Nabber retreated into the shadow of his hat and Beady turned round to face the constable, turning Rocky round with him. But though Rocky might

41

be afraid of a ghost, he wasn't afraid of the scuffers. They owed him because he once caught a big crook for them called Jim Simpson, *and* a terrorist!

He dropped down from Beady's shoulders. "Not doin' nothin'," he retorted.

"What were yer tryin' ter get over that wall for then?"

"Wasn't gettin' over it. Lookin' over it."

"Oh yes. This a new hobby of yours, lookin' over walls? Just lookin'? Nothin' else in mind?"

It was then that Billy, thinking fast, said quietly, "We saw a man coming over that wall a few minutes ago, so Rocky thought we should see what was going on."

"What man?"

Rocky rubbed a hand through his red hair angrily. "Just a man – we don't know who he is! He dropped over and ran. Listen, scuffer, we're not doin' nothin' – just tryin' ter find out what the man was doin' that jumped over the wall!"

"Can you describe him?"

"Oh yes," said Rocky sarcastically. "We're de Cats Gang and we can see in der dark!"

"That's enough of that. Off home, all of you, and I don't want to catch yer round here again."

"Come if we want to. S'not private property, this alley, is it? 'Cos if it is, it should have a sign up! Come on, Cats!" And Rocky, hunching his shoulders, angry and virtuous, led the way, commenting, "Try ter do the right thing and they want ter nick yer!"

42

"What's over der wall, den?" asked the Nabber, following. "Dracula, is it?"

Rocky didn't answer straight away, because he was thinking about it. Then he said, "No. S'not Dracula, but maybe it could be a ghost after all."

"Could be," said Beady. "Think it is. It's a old man—"

"Yes, an' he just stands and stares at yer."

"What yer expect him ter do? Wave at yer like the Prince of Wales?" asked the Nabber. "Right waste of time this has been – you and yer sussin'. Sussed out a ghost, did yer? Lotta cod!"

"I'm goin' ter *do* you, Nabber, you *and* yer hat! Think yer J.R., don't yer? And yer know what happened ter *him*!"

From the shadow of his hat the Nabber replied, "Nothin' happens ter *him*. He always *wins*!"

"Well, *you* don't!"

They were in Crown Street, and they felt safe, because that was the end of the Crown Street Gang's territory.

"Hi," said Rocky, relaxing, "dey didn't come after us, the Crown Street lot. Knew dey wouldn't. Dey're all cowards. Like our Joey."

"Go on," said the Nabber. "They couldn't come after us. Murky Evans and his gang's in youth custody for selling smack."

Rocky was shaken. "How d'yer know that?"

"Like me dad said, 'Keep yer lines of communication open if yer goin' ter be a leader.' I've got me lines open. What happened to yours? Got them in a twist?

Havin' us creepin' round scared stiff! And then gettin' scared by a ghost – a ghost!" And the Nabber stood straight and tall.

It was a bad moment for Rocky, and the Cats knew it. The Nabber had really got the better of him.

But then Rocky said, "Yer a real good skin, you are. Get yer kicks out of foolin' yer mates, do yer?"

The Nabber measured up for a fight. "Easy, isn't it? When dey're fools anyway!"

"Right, Nabber."

Rocky put his fists up, but just then Beady said, "Hi – look at that – over der!"

He was pointing to the front door of the house whose backyard wall they had looked over. The door was open, and Constable McMahon was talking to somebody inside. They couldn't see who, but then he looked out at them – a tall man.

"Dat's him," whispered Rocky. "Dat's him. The man at the window wasn't a ghost."

"Thought yer said the place was empty," said the Nabber.

"Could still be a ghost," whispered Beady. "Dey can do anything."

Then the man went inside and McMahon followed him, but before the door was shut behind them, something small and dark dashed out of the house and ran down the street towards the alley.

"It's a rat!" shouted the Nabber. "It'll have ter be exterminated!"

"What for, but?" asked Rocky.

"Disease, that's what for. Dey carry disease!"

44

"Well, with that hat yer should be able to exterminate it with yer gun. Der has ter be a gun ter go with der hat!"

The Cats fell about laughing – even Billy laughed, though he wasn't feeling all that happy. But the Nabber only said, impressively, "Yes. The gun is comin'. It's a Colt."

They didn't have a lot to say as they went towards St Catherine's Square. Billy, Beady and Little Chan were thinking that even though they didn't like the Nabber all that much, he *had* known more about the Crown Street Gang's set-up than Rocky had, they didn't think Rocky would ever get into that house and anyway they were very worried about doing any place in the Crown Street Gang's territory, even if they were in youth custody as the Nabber had said. Rocky was stalking ahead, feeling furious and defeated, but determined to get into that house and show the Nabber he couldn't take over the Cats. The Nabber followed behind, thinking about the Colt.

When they got into the Square, the Cats hung about, undecided about things – except for Rocky.

"Listen," he said. "We'll get inter that place – tellin' yer – make a fortune!"

"But *how*, Rocky?" asked Beady.

"Leave dat ter me!" and not knowing what else to do – he felt he had to do something to liven things up – he leapt on to the wall round the abandoned garden and started running round it, arms stretched out, and shouting, "Come on – we'll go ter the hideout!"

But it didn't work, because the only result was that a window was flung open on the other side of the Square, and a voice shouted, "That you, Beady Martin? You not home in two minutes, I'll batter yer!"

"S'me mam," said Beady. "Have ter go," and he departed hastily.

"Me also," said Little Chan.

"See youse," said the Nabber, detached, and drifted off.

"Yer a rotten lot!" shouted Rocky, so Billy stayed on to say,

"Forget about the Nabber, Rocky."

"Doesn't bother *me*!"

"Tell yer what, Rocky. Don't think it was a burglar that came over the wall at that house. He didn't have nothin' with him."

"Yer right, Billy. What I'm sayin'. He was just sussin' der place, which means it's worth doin', like I said."

"But there *is* somebody living there."

"All right – de old feller. No problem, and he's got a lot of good loot there. Yer comin' ter the hideout?"

Billy had had enough experience for one day, and he wasn't happy about cycling home in the dark, anyway.

"Sorry, Rocky. Have ter get back," he said. "See yer."

As Rocky watched the tail light of his tricycle moving away towards St Catherine's Buildings, he

46

felt deserted. Nothing to do but go home. The funny thing was, he realised as he took a last look round the Square, that although St Catherine's Buildings stood up like a big liner with all its port-holes lit up on one side, and most of the old terraced houses on the other side of the Square had lights shining through their curtains, the curtains downstairs at Number 3 were still open and there was no light inside, only a red glow. And Joey's bike was still parked outside.

At first sight, the living room looked a bit like Aladdin's cave, because the electric fire was going full blast, causing the red glow Rocky had seen outside, and a pale shaft of light from the street lamp came in through the window from the Square. Apart from that, the room was shadowy and silent.

Rocky switched on the light, and everything re-turned to normal: the carpet with the hole in it, the lumpy sofa, the bed in its usual rumpled state, the blankets twisted into a kind of horizontal column, and the dark alcove where the gas cooker was. He went to close the curtains and fastened them together with the safety-pin, wondering where Suzie had got to, and whether she'd run off again. As he turned away from the window his brother Joey, who'd been slumped in the chair beside the fire, turned round and asked nerv-ously, "Who's it?"

"S'me. What yer been in the dark for?"

"Hello dur, skin," said Joey weakly.

"Wur's me mam?"

"Haven't seen her."

"Wur's Suzie? With me mam, is she?"

"I wuddent know."

"Just got back from de moon, have yer?"

Then a voice from behind the sofa whispered, "Rocky." It was Suzie, her face small and pale, looking over at him.

"Yer rubbish," said Rocky, exasperated. "What yer doin' behind der?"

"Him," whispered Suzie, as though Joey was Frankenstein's monster.

"He won't hurt yer."

Suzie stood up and peered over the sofa at Joey.

"What's up wid *her*?" Joey asked. "What's she doin' der? Didn't know she was der—"

"Frightened of yer. Yer know that."

"What she frightened of me for, but? Done her no harm," said Joey, aggrieved.

"She was here when yer battered her dad, wasn't she?"

"I never battered. . ."

"Yer did – *and* yer took me mam's money. Steal off yer mam and yer hand'll drop off!"

For some reason that started Joey groaning, and he turned away towards the fire.

Rocky wondered what was wrong with him. Wasn't like Joey.

"How's der job goin'?" he asked, conversationally, but Joey only shook his head.

"When yer goin' den?" he insisted. "Back wherever yer come from? When yer get the job done?"

48

Joey turned on him fiercely. "Listen, kid, I'll do yer if yer don't shurrup!"

"Oh yes, like yer did that big crook Jim Simpson that chased yer round Lodge Lane and that I had ter rescue yer from?"

Joey stood up threateningly, but just then there was a knock at the door and a voice said, "Constable McMahon here. Mind if I come in?"

Joey went the colour of one of Mrs Flanagan's sheets and sat down, while Suzie dropped behind the sofa.

"Dey got somethin' on yer, the scuffers?" whispered Rocky. Joey shook his head, and Rocky went to open the door. "What's it?" he asked, but not letting the policeman in.

"That man yer saw coming over the wall, Rocky. Can yer give me any more information – about what he looked like?" He added, not missing anything, since he was a scuffer, "See yer brother's back. How's things, Joey?"

Joey shot out of his chair like a rocket from NASA and chuntered, "All right, yer know like."

"He's as right as a burst bag of wind," said Rocky. "And dat feller that come over der wall – he was sort of medium like. Think his hair was brownish, and he had a dark jacket and jeans, and he hurt himself comin' over der wall. Could of been the glass. Yer could find some of his blood on der ground," he added with relish.

"Proper Sherlock, aren't yer?" said Constable McMahon.

49

"Did he get anythin', that feller?" asked Rocky, interested.

"Not this time. And you can forget the whole thing, and don't try looking over the wall again."

"What's all dis? What's goin' on?" Rocky's mother pushed past the constable, bristling with anxiety and anger. "What yer doin' here? It's prosecution, that's what it is. I'm goin' ter see the Militants about it."

"That's up ter you, Mrs Flanagan. I'm just making some inquiries. Nothing ter do with any of *you*."

"Should think not!" Then, suspiciously, Mrs Flanagan asked, "Nothin' ter do with Rocky, is it? He's not got inter somethin'?"

"Shurrup, mam!" hissed Rocky. It was stupid to put ideas into a scuffer's head.

"Right, Rocky – if yer remember anything else. . . 'Night, Mrs Flanagan. Take care, Joey." And McMahon departed.

"The nurve!" exclaimed Mrs Flanagan, when he'd gone. "Who's he think he is, comin' in here and askin' questions? Prosecution, that's what it is. Dey always picks on us!" and she collapsed into her chair and kicked her shoes off. "Yer all right, Joey? Are yer hungry? There's nothin' much in, but I made a bit on the 'ousey, so we'll splash out. What yer fancy? Rocky, yer can go down ter Pa Richardson's and get some—"

"I'm not gettin' any pies," said Rocky, firmly.

"I didn't say nothin' about pies! You mind yer lip! Yer'll eat what yer given." She thought the matter

50

over. "Yer can get a few slices of ham and a big tin of peas, and yer can get two lots of chips at Chan's. That do yer, Joey?" And she went to find her purse and a plastic carrier bag.

Joey looked round at Rocky and said, quietly and anxiously, "What was all that? With der scuffer? That business about the wall and somebody comin' over?"

"Was in the alley leadin' inter Crown Street. There's this wall with broken glass on top, and somebody come over. . ."

"The scuffer seen him?"

"No – the scuffer come after. . ."

"Sure about that?"

"Course I am."

Joey sank back in the chair and turned towards the fire, and Rocky began to wonder about him. It wasn't like Joey be flattened. But then he remembered Joey scared stiff and hiding in the old gravel yard behind the Cathedral when Jim Simpson was after him. What was Joey into? Couldn't have been, could it, Joey coming over that wall?

"Hi, Joey—" he said, but then his mother interrupted.

"That's a fiver, Rocky. An' I'll want the change."

Rocky prepared to bargain. "What do I get for goin', but?"

"My hand across yer face if yer don't get off !"

Rocky stood his ground. "Cakes," he said.

Mrs Flanagan weakened. "Two cakes," she conceded. "Small ones. We could halve them. It doesn't grow on trees, yer know. And der's been nothin' from Flanagan," she added, reflectively.

"Yer comin', Suzie?" asked Rocky.

They went down the dark Steps that led to Larkspur Lane, Suzie clutching the sleeve of Rocky's anorak. "Listen," he said, as they approached Pa Richardson's grocery, "behave yerself in here an' leave it ter me, see?"

Suzie nodded solemnly and followed him into the shop. But Pa Richardson wasn't there. Instead, there was a rather plump man in a white coat behind the counter, leaning casually on the shelves behind him, his arms crossed over his chest, and observing them with a steady, knowing look – a lot different from Pa Richardson bumbling round like a short-sighted and underfed bee.

Rocky stopped dead. "Wur's Pa Richardson?"

"Not so well. I'm lookin' after things for him. I'm his nephew."

Rocky was stunned for a moment. Generally he relied on being able to do Pa Richardson for something, but he'd have to rethink his tactics now. He studied Pa Richardson's nephew.

"Can I get yer somethin'?" asked the nephew, with sarcastic politeness.

"I want four slices of ham cut thin, and a big tin of peas," said Rocky fiercely.

"Right." Pa Richardson's nephew put the ham on the slicing machine and said in an offhand way, "Will yer keep *her* under control? She's got her hand in the Cola Bottle sweets. S'all right if yer goin' ter pay

52

for what she takes, mind. And d'yer want garden or marrowfat?"

"What yer mean?"

"The kind of peas yer want. That's four thin slices, right?"

"Dey're thin as sheets of paper!"

"Well, you asked for them and they're cut now, and yer lucky ter have them cut fresh and not wrapped up in plastic. Me uncle's a century behind things, yer know. I could make this place inter a super little Spar shop. And a big tin of peas, marrowfat, right? And she's got her hands into the Beastly Wobblies now. . ."

He fixed wide, steady eyes on Suzie who, with her handful of sweets gripped tightly, glared at him and said fiercely, "You swine!"

That shook Pa Richardson's nephew – it even shook Rocky – and he took a step backwards. "*What* did she say?"

"You swine!" Suzie repeated, even more fiercely.

"Disgustin'," said Pa Richardson's nephew, "ter hear that kind of language from the lips of a child!"

"She doesn't mean it, yer know like. She doesn't understand what she's sayin'. Don't know where she picks it up. Drop dem sweets, Suzie, and shurrup!" said Rocky. He'd never had to cope with this sort of situation in Pa Richardson's before, and he was angry at being pushed round and was thinking rapidly. Casually he said, "Hi, an' I'll have some of dem sweets – the toffees – on der top shelf."

It had never failed with Pa Richardson, because he always went to get the step-ladder and climb up and bring the jar down, during which time Rocky had always been able to nick a cake or a couple of biscuits from the counter. But the nephew was up to that sort of thing.

"Them?" He looked up at the jar on the top shelf. "Got some of them down here under the counter. Saves the legs."

As he weighed out a quarter, Rocky scowled. Must have come over on a razor boat, he thought.

"Right," he said. "What yer chargin' for dese cakes?"

"Same as always – ten pence each."

"Rip off! Dey've been here since Noah's Ark unloaded dem at Albert Dock!"

"Yer don't *have* ter buy them. So that's the ham and the peas and a quarter of toffees and them Cola Bottles and Beastly Wobblies yer sister took, which is another—"

"Bad!" spluttered Suzie.

"Right, in't she?" Pa Richardson's nephew smiled widely. "So that'll be two pounds ten. Unless yer want the cakes."

Out in Larkspur Lane, Rocky vowed he would do Pa Richardson's nephew yet.

They were just going up the Steps, having got the chips at Chan's, when Suzie said, "Rocky!" and pointed upwards.

It was the nutter again, coming down towards them. Rocky pulled Suzie back into Larkspur Lane and across the road to hide in the doorway of the chippy, but when the man got to the bottom of the Steps he stopped and pointed at them and said,

"You're there!" and then walked on.

Rocky and Suzie stayed still, waiting until he was out of sight. Then Rocky said, "Come on, Suzie. It's safe."

"Not safe!" And Suzie pulled back into the doorway.

"Tellin' yer it's safe – come on!"

"Devil!" shouted Suzie.

"Der's no devils dese days – have ter be a wizard!" But he thought he knew who the man was – the one who lived in that house with the rats – the Ratman! And he remembered what Suzie said had frightened her into hiding in Princes Gate Hotel: "Black and white an' up there." She must have seen the Ratman through one of the windows – and the Ratman must have seen *him* looking in.

Mrs Flanagan was sitting in her chair, staring into the electric fire. She didn't show much interest in them. "Yer back, then," she said.

"Listen, mam, der was this old feller – the one on the Steps – an' he's crazy or somethin', an' I think. . ."

She didn't seem to hear him. "Joey's gone," she said, tragically. "Yer might as well not of got all that stuff."

"Why not, but? We can have it – there'll be more for us." Rocky opened the tin of peas and put them in a pan on the cooker to warm up. "These is marrowfat," he said. "All right? And Pa Richardson. . ."

"Tell yer, Rocky," went on Mrs Flanagan, "der's somethin' wrong with Joey. It's worryin' me. Don't know what it is. Not just his hand."

55

"Always been somethin' wrong wid Joey," said Rocky, getting the plates.

"What yer mean?" asked Mrs Flanagan indignantly. "He's always been a good son ter me."

"What yer give him when he went? All yer winnin's on the housey?"

"Give him a few pounds."

"That's all right, then. Nothin' ter worry about." Rocky was sharing out the chips and ham. "He'll be back when he's spent it. Fetch the peas over her, will yer, tatty-'ead, and get a spoon for dem."

"I'm not havin' anythin' said against Joey!" exclaimed Mrs Flanagan.

"Ah, come on, mam! The chips is gettin' soggy!"

Mrs Flanagan sat down at the table, looking down at the food on her plate as if it wasn't there. Suzie wasted no time. She started eating the peas first. Suzie always ate the peas first if there were some. Rocky started on the chips.

Mrs Flanagan sighed, ate a chip and said, "Yes, he'll come back. Poor lad – and him with that hand."

It wasn't until they'd got to the point where Suzie had started to manufacture a ham and chip butty and Rocky had nearly finished, that something occurred to him that took his mind off the telly. Why had Joey left? And why was he in such a funny mood? After all, he was supposed to be into a good thing. And why had he been so nervous with McMahon?

"What was wrong wid his hand? Joey's?" he asked.

"Cut it." Mrs Flanagan got up to fill the kettle. "Nasty cut it was."

56

"What'd he cut it on?"

"Somethin' ter do with mendin' the bike."

No, it wasn't the bike, Rocky decided. He'd been right. It *had* been Joey coming over that wall, and he'd cut his hand on the glass. And that was why McMahon scared him, and why he'd been groaning. *That* was the job: that house – but he hadn't got in! So the sooner *he* got into it, the better! And he was just deciding to suss it out again when his mother, dropping her knife and fork, flopped back in her chair, staring at the opposite wall.

"I've got the intuitions somethin' awful!" she moaned.

Rocky and Suzie watched her apprehensively. Mrs Flanagan's intuitions were well known in the family, and when she said something was going to happen it generally did.

"What yer got the intuitions about?" Rocky asked anxiously.

"Don't know." Mrs Flanagan closed her eyes.

"'Bout Flanagan?"

She shook her head.

"Joey?"

Mrs Flanagan opened her eyes. "No," she said, pointing at Suzie. "It's about her! Her!"

Suzie immediately threw the remains of her butty at her stepmother. Mrs Flanagan started up, brushing pieces of bread and chips and ham from her jumper and shouted, "I'll batter yer for that!" Suzie slid off the sofa and under the table, and Mrs Flanagan grabbed the long-handled brush from the corner beside the cooker and began attacking Suzie with it under the table. Rocky hauled Suzie out and dragged her, shrieking hysterically, into the other room.

"Will yer belt up, Suzie!" he said urgently. "Will yer shurrup! Yer makin' things worse!"

Suzie glared at him. "Witch!"

"All right den. But shurrup! Here, get yerself into Joey's bed – he'll not be needin' it, and I'll get yer another butty. All right?"

Suzie glared for another few minutes, then got herself under the blankets on Joey's bed and pulled them over her head.

As he went through the passage from one room to the next, Rocky heard a voice from above say, "Rocky." It was Ellen-from-upstairs looking anxiously over the banisters, her long blonde hair falling over her face.

"Hello, dur," said Rocky. "How's it?"

"Can yer keep things a bit quiet, Rocky? Like yer mam and Suzie? It bothers me husband, the noise, see."

"Could get him some ear-plugs."

"Mean it, Rocky."

"Right den." Ellen vanished, but then her husband came down the stairs, walking in a dignified way and wearing a grey city suit, the one he'd worn at their wedding, when Mrs Flanagan had done them a wedding tea.

"How's things?" asked Rocky.

"How d'yer think they are, living above you lot?"

He had the smallest, meanest blue eyes Rocky had ever seen, and he remembered now that at the wedding tea *he'd* been the only one to notice the cobwebs above the cooker that Mrs Flanagan had missed when she was cleaning the place up. Fancy Dan, he was, thought Rocky, and he asked with false humility, "You der new Lord Mayor, den?"

"Clear off!" Ellen's husband strode through the passage, only slightly inconvenienced by Rocky's foot, which accidentally got in his way.

Mrs Flanagan was sitting in an unusual silence. The telly wasn't going, and she was staring at the electric fire. She didn't even turn round as he came in.

Rocky gave her a wary look, and started putting together some ham and chip butties. They were cold, the chips. "Ellen's feller was on der stairs," he said, "an' he's complainin' about der noise again."

He was hoping to distract his mother's attention from Suzie, but she only said gloomily, "She should never of married him. Yer should never get married!"

Getting desperate, Rocky buttered more bread and asked, "Yer want der telly on?"

"I don't know. I do me best lookin' after things, and *her*" (meaning Suzie) "and yer get a card and den nothin'. An' what yer always on *her* side for?" Mrs Flanagan demanded angrily. "She threw things at me – yer saw that. At yer *mother*! An' yer take her part. One thing about Joey, he always takes *my* part."

59

"Well, yer always gives him money, don't yer?" muttered Rocky.

"What's that yer say?"

"Here, mam." Rocky put a butty in front of her, and was relieved when she started to eat it. "I'll put the kettle on," he said, then, hoping her mood had changed, "Listen, mam, Suzie's just a tiddler, yer know like, an' she doesn't know what's happenin' an' she gets scared. . . An' Flanagan'll come back. He'll have to. For Suzie." Then he knew he'd said the wrong thing, and quickly gave her a cup of tea.

Mrs Flanagan drank it, thoughtfully, then she said, "Whatever happens, when Flanagan comes back – *if* he does – he'll have ter put *her* in a home. I'm not havin' it any longer."

"Yer can't do that ter Suzie," Rocky protested. "Would kill her."

Mrs Flanagan sat back in her chair. "Not any longer," she repeated. "She's not my flesh and blood. And she's mental. I knew it when I married Flanagan. I was thinking in the middle of the service, I'm takin' a stick ter me own back, takin' that girl on. An' I've been proved right!"

As Rocky tried to get to sleep, he couldn't put out of his mind his mother's angry face, framed by black curls, her eyes fierce. She wasn't really bad, his mam, she just got things wrong – like thinking Joey had a halo round his head, and Suzie had come from the other place. But she couldn't put Suzie into a home.

60

Flanagan wouldn't let her anyway. But what if he didn't come back?

Only thing to do, he decided, was to get into that house before Joey did, so that he'd have some money, and if necessary him and Suzie could run off somewhere. He couldn't think where, but there had to be somewhere. Maybe London. First thing was to get into that house. And suddenly he had an idea for doing it.

CHAPTER

4

The most exotic figure at morning break next day was the Nabber, propped up against the wall in his ten-gallon hat, looking like a relaxed, top-heavy lamp-post in a leaning position.

"Hi, listen, Nabber," said Rocky, dancing about a bit to get warm, "'bout dis house. . ."

The Nabber didn't even look at him. He was obviously self-engrossed and reluctant to communicate with anybody about anything.

"Nabber - der's things ter discuss . . ." It made no impression. Rocky went over to the rest of the Cats. "Think we should have the cremation soon," he concluded.

"There's life there yet but," said Billy.

"Not a lot," said Beady.

"Didn't mean the Nabber, meant the hat," said Rocky, and the Cats fell about laughing. "D'yer think it's a brain-blocker?"

"It must be a brain-insulator," said Little Chan, and was pleased when the Cats fell about again.

"Have ter get through to him," said Rocky, but a group had started gathering round the Nabber, so the Cats moved away. You could never tell what might happen – the Nabber's hat excited either admiration or hostility in the on-lookers.

"Got the Allsorts booked, Rocky," said Billy. "Saturday morning. Had a word with their captain. . ."

"Great," said Rocky absent-mindedly.

"Let the wingy know?" When Rocky didn't answer, Billy sensed that Rocky wasn't really interested, but he'd gone to a lot of trouble over the match. "They seem all right, but I don't know – could be trouble."

"Great," repeated Rocky. "An' listen, I've got a idea for gettin' into that house. Got it all worked out. . ."

"The house with der ghost?" asked Beady.

"Not a ghost, but," said Rocky. "He's alive. He's the Ratman."

Unexpectedly, Beady said, "I don't *want* ter get into it. Don't like it. So yer can ferget about me!"

Rocky could hardly believe it. "Well, yer'll not gerra share of the loot!"

"Rocky," said Beady solemnly, "I don't *care!*"

Rocky shrugged, pretending *he* didn't care. "Up ter you. That leaves Billy an' Little Chan an'. . ."

But it was obvious that Billy and Little Chan felt the same.

Rocky was disgusted. "Yer wuddent believe it! Ferget it den! Youse lot is as useful as Barbie dolls when it comes ter anythin' important! Der only one yer can rely on is the Nabber – he's a good skin!" Which the other Cats didn't believe was true. Neither did Rocky, for that matter, but he had to have somebody with him. "If any of youse can get through ter the Nabber," he went on, "tell him termorrer at the

Crown Street house – after school. An' I'm *finished* wid you lot!"

"Doesn't know what he's gettin' inter," said Beady, as Rocky stalked away.

"Wish he'd listened about the Allsorts," said Billy.

Rocky had no further communication with the Cats that day, but as he was leaving school a voice behind him said, "Hi – you Rocky O'Rourke?"

Rocky turned round. It was the cave-insect boy who'd been watching him when he was sussing the Ratman's, looking thinner than ever.

"What yer want?"

"Yer *are* Rocky O'Rourke?"

"Course I am."

"Had to make sure. Everybody said yer were, but – had to – got dis for yer," and he held out an envelope, an expensive-looking, long, white envelope.

Rocky looked at it suspiciously, reluctant to take it. "What's dis? Dis a summons?"

But the boy pushed it into his hand and ran off. Rocky opened the envelope. The sheet of paper inside was also expensive-looking, not like the paper his mother used when she occasionally corresponded. What was more, the message was typewritten. It said: "Keep away from the Ratman. He is my property."

As he stood, frowning and putting the paper back in the envelope, a tall, black boy with dreadlocks under a red woolly cap, balancing on skates, was looking at him through a rolled-up sheet of paper like a telescope.

64

"What yer up to, 'Nelson'?" Rocky demanded, but the boy didn't answer. "Here – you got somethin' ter do wid this?" He waved the envelope at the black boy, but he still didn't move, so Rocky started towards him. Then the boy said, "Trouble comin'. Goin' ter be trouble," and skated off.

Trouble coming, Rocky thought, as he ran along Princes Boulevard, hopping over puddles and uneven paving stones. He didn't need to be told it was coming – he had it already. Who was behind the cave insect? Who had sent him that letter? Somebody else with his eye on the loot in that house – but *he* seemed to own the Ratman. And what help was *he* getting from the Cats? Wasn't on, he thought. All left to me!

It just happened that the 'Beatles City Tour' bus had broken down on the Boulevard and was marooned by the kerb, the driver with his head under the bonnet and an assortment of tourists on the pavement being guarded by a female courier with a clipboard, while the wind engulfed them in a surge of dust and assorted litter. The tourists had a look of wealth about them that took Rocky's thoughts from his immediate problems and drew him like a magnet.

He approached the courier first, as a means of getting into the action.

"Want a push, missus?" he asked.

"Clear off !" she said quietly but threateningly out of the side of her mouth, having immediately recognised Rocky's nuisance potential.

"Just thought yer might like a push with the bus."

65

"This Beatle country as well?" asked a tall American, looking round at the old houses.

With an anxious glance at the disabled bus, the courier pushed Rocky aside. "Well," she said, "this is certainly Liverpool 8 and certainly—"

Rocky seized his opportunity, and got in front of the courier, gazing up at the American, an eager and helpful expression on his face. "Yer lookin' for der Beatles' places, mister?" he asked. "'Cos I used ter know them."

"*You* did, son?" The American focused down on Rocky's red hair in some surprise. "How come you—"

"Don't be stupid," snapped the courier, losing her calm. "You're too young to have known the Beatles!"

"You callin' me a liar, missus?" demanded Rocky indignantly, his eyes fierce as a tiger's. "I'll have me dad on ter yer! Didn't say I knew der Beatles!"

"Clear off then," said the courier. Rocky hesitated, thinking he might have got into something he couldn't cope with, but determined to go on.

"S'like dis. Was me brother Joey. Was a friend of Paul's, an' he come round ter see us when he was back in Liverpool – at St Catherine's Square. Could show yer. Could show yer der chair he used ter sit in. An' every time," he paused as he came, perilously, to the final try, "every time he come he shook my hand."

"Paul McCartney shook your hand?"

"Dat's right!" Rocky relaxed, seeing that he had got through, because the American was ignoring the courier. "Don't really remember it but, yer know. Was only a tiddler, see. But me brother's told me all about

66

it. An' yer shouldn't listen to her," indicating the courier. "She knows nothin' about it. Just me brother an' me knows. . ."

"Can I meet your brother?"

"He's away jus' now," said Rocky hastily.

"But I could shake your hand? My grandson would appreciate it if he could know that I had shaken the hand that Paul McCartney shook."

"Yer can shake it." Rocky rubbed his hand down the leg of his jeans. "Only thing is, I have ter charge, see? If I didn't, me hand would be shook off. Like the Duke of Edinburgh's."

"I didn't know the Duke of Edinburgh had lost a hand. . ."

"Not lost it really. Only it's critical. An' secret jus' now."

Rocky was sweating, and as the American was obviously having doubts he said quickly, "Just charge two pounds a shake. . ."

"I don't think I've ever come across a bigger little conman. . ."

"Now, listen, mister. . ."

"So here's the two pounds, and let's shake, and my friend here will take the photograph."

With the round pounds in his left hand, Rocky shook hands with his right, grinning into the camera, then he shoved off fast.

He was jubilant. Easiest two he'd ever made. And he could join the Baptist Youth Club now – he had his subs!

★

67

The message *had* got through to the Nabber, because he was waiting for Rocky beside the house in Crown Street. He was laconic and chewing, and Rocky had his football under his arm.

"Right then," said the Nabber. "What's the big plan dis time? Yer gettin' inter the house or playin' footy?"

"Both. It's footy against the wall, see?"

"What yer on about?"

"We're playin' footy against the wall, and then the ball goes over. Then we ring the doorbell and say, 'Can we get de ball, mister? It's gone inter your yard.' An' *he* says, 'Course yer can, lads,' and 'Come in' an' we go in an ' we suss der place as we go through – the locks an' everythin', and—"

"What if he's not in?" asked the Nabber.

"He will be. The wingy told me. He only goes out after dark."

The Nabber, looking reflectively across at the house, asked, "What if he doesn't open the door?"

"Think up another possibility!" exclaimed Rocky in exasperation. "The enthusiasm is mind-shatterin'! Why don't *you* come up wid an idea? Yer *never* come up with *anythin'*!"

The Nabber shrugged. "No need to wid you around. One a minute, you are."

"Listen," said Rocky, "our Joey's interested in di place – it's the job he's plannin'."

"Yer sure?"

"He was the one come over der wall. Somethin else," he added, and handed the Nabber the letter he'c

68

received. The Nabber took it over to the street lamp to read it. He was obviously impressed.

"This from your Joey?" he asked.

"Cuddent be. Our Joey cuddent put one word in front of another."

The Nabber reflected. "Looks like half Liverpool's goin' ter do this place," he concluded, "you, your Joey, this feller that wrote the letter and Murky Evans, if they let him out in time. Think yer could be inter gang warfare."

"But *we'll* be first in, see? Ah, come on! Are yer givin' it a try?"

"Right."

"Right!" Rocky bounced the football and kicked it against the wall. The Nabber retrieved it and sent it back again. Rocky retrieved it and kicked it back.

"Gettin' boring," said the Nabber, his hat wobbling as he gave the ball another kick.

"Next one goes over!" Rocky lifted the ball and it disappeared over the glass-topped wall, and they stood listening to the sound of it bouncing.

"Well," commented the Nabber, "Flanagan might get yer another one."

"Shurrup!" Rocky went to the front door of the house and pressed the bell. He didn't know what might happen – anything could. It made you sweat, and he clenched his fists tightly. But nothing happened.

"Told yer," said the Nabber.

Rocky pressed the bell again, and thought he saw somebody moving behind one of the coloured glass windows at the side of the door. So he pressed again – still no answer.

Then the Nabber shouted, "Rocky!" and as the football came back over the wall and bounced down the street they heard somebody laughing behind the wall, and a voice said,

"There's try and fail!"

"I'm clearin' off. This is spooky!" said the Nabber.

But Rocky thought that the old man behind the wall was nobody's fool and had seen through his plan, so he shouted back, "Der's win and lose – thanks very much, mister!" He knew he had a difficult job on.

"Yer dealin' with a nutter, and he's barricaded himself in, and yer not goin' ter get in!" the Nabber said when they got to St Catherine's Square, and he went off home.

"I'll get in!" Rocky shouted after him. "I'll get in!"

"Yer all mouth!" was the Nabber's parting shot.

"Can't do nothin', so yer wear a big hat!" was Rocky's.

His voice echoed round the empty Square as the Nabber disappeared, and Rocky pushed his hand through his red hair so that it stood on end. He felt, in spite of what he'd been saying, that he'd failed and that he wouldn't ever get into that house. He glowered at the Anglican Cathedral, and it glowered back at him, seeming to be saying to him, disgustedly, "You wic der big 'ead!"

Rocky sat down on the doorstep of Number 3 elbows on his knees, face in his fists, and though about it. There had to be some way of getting into that house. Then he had an idea. He knew the old man only went out after dark, so the first thing was to follow him, and time him, so that he could find out when the house was empty. Then it was just a matter of getting in, even if it meant breaking a window. And if he'd got it planned, the Cats would come in with him, he was sure. But who'd written the letter the cave insect had given him? And when was Joey planning *his* move?

"'Lo der, Rocky," said a voice beside him. "Can I get past yer?"

It was Ellen-from-upstairs, pushing Trevor in his pram. She put the brake on the pram, got a basket of groceries from off Trevor's feet and shook her long blonde hair back from her face.

"How's things? Yer all right?"

Rocky stood up and kicked an empty beer can across the pavement. "Could be better, yer know like."

"Yer right there." She sounded very unhappy.

"Trevor all right?" he asked, to take her mind off things.

"He's all right," she said, as she hoisted him out of the pram.

"Help yer wid yer things?"

"Can manage."

"How's yer feller?"

With Trevor on one arm and the bag of groceries in her other hand, Ellen went into Number 3. "Never get married, Rocky," she said.

Rocky was slightly stunned. "Wasn't thinkin' of it."

"An' Suzie. She's in the launderette, top of Joseph Terrace."

"In the. . .? What's she doin' der? Me mam wid her?"

"By herself," said Ellen, meaningly, and went upstairs.

Suzie *was* in the launderette. After all, it was warm in there, and you could watch the washing going round in the machines as you crouched in a pre-formed plastic chair. And you were safe from the world there, because nobody came in except to sit and watch their washing going round in the machines.

"Tatty-'ead!" said Rocky. "What yer doin' in here?"

Suzie looked up at him, scowling. She didn't speak, and Rocky could tell she was in a state. She didn't even seem to know him. And there was a bruise on her cheek.

He sat down beside her. "Who battered yer, Suzie?" he asked.

Suzie just watched the washing.

"Yer know *her*?" asked the woman attendant, coming up to them.

"Me stepsister."

"Well, yer'd better get her home. She's been sittin' there for hours. Shouldn't be out by herself !"

"Take her home. Come on, Suzie."

Suzie pulled back. "Not come."

"Listen, tatty-'ead, yer comin' wid me!"

If there was one thing Suzie was good at, it was creating an incident. They were very conspicuous as he dragged her along Princes Boulevard, shouting.

72

"What's der matter, Suzie? What happened? Was it me mam? Did she batter yer?"

Suzie sat down firmly on the pavement.

"Look, Suzie," he began desperately, trying to pull her up, but she'd obviously been stuck with Super-Glue.

"Not go back!" she yelled, and added ferociously, "Batter *her*!"

"What yer doin' ter that child?" demanded a voice. It was the old woman in the red woolly hat who lived on Princes Boulevard, the one Rocky had saved from the tiddlers in Joseph Terrace and had got a free ticket for the Baptist Youth Club's Old People's Christmas Tea for – and he'd had no thanks for that!

"Listen, missus—" he began, but she went on.

"I know you! You're the one that batters his sister! Leave that child alone!"

It was definitely going to be an incident. He considered things. You could never make Suzie do something she didn't want to.

"Go ter the hideout, Suzie," he suggested desperately.

Suzie thought about this for a moment. Then she got up and turned to the old woman in the red woolly cap and said, "You swine!"

"Well! Of all the. . .!"

"S'nothin' personal, missus," said Rocky hastily. "Everybody's swine to her just now." As he dragged her along, he shouted, "Get somethin' ter eat from Pa Richardson's, Suzie. All right?"

"Beastly Wobblies, an' Cola Bottles, an' crisps an' a orange!" Suzie shouted back, obviously seeking compensation for Mrs Flanagan's battering. Then she added, "Bubble gum!"

Just as well I met the Beatle seekers, Rocky thought.

Pa Richardson's nephew did not welcome them, but he did not refuse to serve them. He just kept his eyes on them while he counted out the Beastly Wobblies and the Cola Bottles, one bubble gum, two cans of orange, two packets of crisps, one smoky bacon, the other cheese and onion, and demanded the money, adding, "An' tell yer sister ter keep her hand out of the False Teeth!"

In the hideout, with one candle lit, Suzie concentrated on eating Beastly Wobblies and Cola Bottles ferociously. Rocky ate crisps. He couldn't bring himself to eat Beastly Wobblies and Cola Bottles, and he was worried about how he was going to persuade Suzie to come home.

At last he asked, "*Did* she batter yer, me mam?"

Suzie frowned and said, "Bad!" and something else she shouldn't have, and ate another Cola Bottle.

Wish Flanagan would get himself back, Rocky thought, watching Suzie chewing gum and blowing out the biggest bubble ever – big enough for the Guinness Book of Records, he thought. Fascinated, he watched her chew it up again, pull out a long line of gum and twist it round into a long rope. Then she chewed it up again, took it out of her mouth, rolled it into a ball, threw it on the floor and

74

then retrieved it, covered with dust, and put it into her mouth again.

"Spit it out, yer rubbish!" Rocky shouted. "It's mucky!"

Suzie glared at him and blew another bubble.

"All right, tatty-'ead, poison yerself," he said, and started clearing up the empty packets. "Listen, we're goin' back home, an' if yer behave yerself, I'll learn yer ter swim."

"In der pond?" asked Suzie enthusiastically, through the chewing-gum.

"In der swimmin' pool! Now, *listen*. We go out of here quietly, an' yer don't make a fuss. Got it?"

Suzie nodded.

"Right. An' I *mean* behave yerself!"

Where's Flanagan, he wondered desperately. Enjoying himself riding in the desert in a long dress on the back of a camel! Should be here!

CHAPTER

5

It was still dark when Rocky woke up next morning, and he lay for a few minutes thinking out what he should do. The first thing was to keep his mother and Suzie apart until the trouble died down.

He got out of bed, and went into the living room. It was dead quiet, apart from the ticking of the alarm clock on the mantelpiece and the sound of his mother's breathing. Cautiously, in the light from the street lamp that came in through the pinned-together curtains, he felt his way to the table and the remains of last night's supper. He buttered a couple of slices of bread, and departed as unobtrusively as a ghost dematerialising.

"Here, tatty-'ead," he said, waking Suzie. "Get dis inter yer, an' den get yer clothes on an' then get off ter school. Got it? Keep clear of me mam, an' don't make a noise."

Suzie started eating the bread and butter, still half asleep. Then she said, "Go wid you."

"Yer *can't*. I've got things on. Now have yer got it, Suzie? What yer goin' ter do?"

"Not see *her*."

"Dat's right."

"Go ter school."

"Dat's right. Yer've got it."

She was all right, really, was Suzie, he concluded as he left the house. You just had to put things to her so that she could understand what you were on about, and then she was all right.

In the half-light outside Rocky, hunched in his anorak, did a bit of running on the spot, to get some circulation going in his feet. Was no good, these trainers, he thought. Worn through, nearly. Maybe Flanagan would buy him a new pair. But he hadn't a lot of faith in Flanagan.

There were some lights in the windows round the Square and in St Catherine's Buildings, the street lights were still on and a faint red tinge in the sky over the Cathedral suggested that there *would* be some daylight soon. Rocky leapt on to the parapet round the abandoned garden, ran along it, jumped off and shot down the Steps to Larkspur Lane. It was a lot more cheerful in the Lane, with the lights from the newsagent's and Pa Richardson's grocery, where his nephew could be seen getting into his white coat in preparation for the day's business, and people were walking fast to catch buses.

The rest of the Cats weren't there yet, and Rocky hopped from one foot to the other to keep warm, and started thinking about that BMX bike he was going to get when he sold the loot from the Ratman's house. He started running round, imagining he was pedalling the bike, did a wheelie, and then a hip-hanger, and was just about to do a bunnyhop when he found he was outside the newsagent's and the woman behind the counter was staring at him. Rocky started reading the various notices stuck on the window, earnestly, as though he were looking out for a secondhand BMX, which in a way he was, but nobody was selling. However, there *was* a notice saying 'Paper boys and girls wanted', which was worth looking into in spite of the fact that the woman leaning her skinny elbows on the counter and puffing cigarette smoke over an order book was an enemy of his. After all, it was always warm in there. He pushed open the door.

"Yer wantin' paper boys, missus?" he asked the woman.

She looked at him suspiciously, her mouth a gash of red lipstick.

"What about it?"

"Go through a lot of dem, do yer? Suppose dey get soggy when it rains?" He knew he shouldn't have said it, but he couldn't resist it.

The woman glared at him. "Now look, you—" she began.

"Sorry, missus. Was just wonderin' what yer pay dem. I might consider der job."

"Well, forget it! I'm not considerin' *you*! Wouldn't trust *you* with a dishcloth, let alone a sack of newspapers. And if yer've come in for nothin', get out!"

"Just come for me comic, but I can take me trade elsewhere."

They glared at each other across the counter, then the woman said, "Get it den, quick! And I'm sorry for anybody yer take yer trade to!"

So Rocky hung about, taking his time over making his selection, though he knew from the start that he would buy the *Eagle*. Then, since a man came in to get a newspaper and had the full attention of the woman as he talked to her – unlike Rocky, he was obviously a valued customer – he slipped a copy of the *Dandy* inside the *Eagle*, because Suzie liked colouring the pages of the *Dandy*, and was particularly interested in the activities of Dinah Mo.

Swiftly he waved the *Eagle* at the woman and dropped twenty-four pence on the counter before she could start inquiries. That'll fix her *and* her paper boys, he thought, and went to lean against the wire frames on the windows of Pa Richardson's shop and read the *Eagle*, while he waited for the rest of the Cats Gang.

He was just sympathising with the Alien Doom-lord's son, Enok, who was being forced by his father to go to school and wondering whether *he* could warp into another identity, as Enok did, when, looking up, he saw a thin figure coming towards him, a figure with a ten-gallon hat on top. It was the Nabber. He's warped himself into a cowboy, Rocky thought.

"Hello, dur. How's things?" he asked.

The Nabber unfastened his jacket to reveal a gun belt slung round his hips, and a gun in the holster.

"Got the Colt," he said, and drawing it pointed it directly at Pa Richardson's nephew who was peering out at them and who immediately disappeared in the direction of the telephone beside the cash register.

"He'll have the jam butty car round in no time," said Rocky in a sympathetic way.

That upset the Nabber. "What for, but?"

"The Colt – yer pointed it at him."

"S'not real but – it's a replica. Doesn't fire, yer know like."

"*He* doesn't know that, but, does he?"

The Nabber reflected on the situation for two seconds and then shot off along Larkspur Lane, his hat in his hand.

"Hi, Nabber!" Rocky shouted after him, understanding the Nabber's predicament. "Yer saggin' school?"

The Nabber did not take time off to stop and turn round – he just raised his arm in confirmation.

"Come wid yer den!" After all, the Nabber would do as much for him.

The Nabber waved again.

"Bus stop – Prinney Boulevard – half an hour?"

The Nabber confirmed this, and disappeared round the corner.

If the thought of a jam butty car scared the Nabber, how would he go into the business of getting rid of the loot from that house, Rocky reflected, and wondered what he'd do with the hat and the gun, but just then the jam butty car *did* arrive, and a policeman got out and confronted Rocky.

"What yer up to?"

"Readin' me comic an' waitin' for me mates."

"Turn yer pockets out."

"What for, but?" Rocky demanded indignantly. "You gorra search warrant?"

"Turn them out. I'll not tell yer again."

Rocky shrugged. "Well, if it'll save yer blood pressure." He folded his comics and stuffed them into the front of his anorak. "But I'll be on ter that lot in Larkspur Lane. Dey owe me, see?" From his pockets he produced the change from the wingy's forty pence and the two round pounds, two biros, a box of matches, a small screwdriver and a packet of Minty's Chewy Mints. The last item worried Rocky. There'd been a warehouse done recently, and a lot of Minty's Mints had been taken and were circulating round the neighbourhood, free – everybody was chewing them. The scuffer might make the connection. But he didn't.

"What's the screwdriver for?" he asked.

"Unscrewing screws."

"What yer carry it for?"

"Well, yer never know. . . Dese things interest yer? Are dey clues?"

"Mind yer lip and come with me." He took Rocky into Pa Richardson's shop, where his nephew was in a state. Knowing that he was innocent, and seeing a way to get his own back, Rocky grinned in a friendly way.

"Hello, der," he said. "All right, are yer?"

"Is this the boy that had the gun?" asked the policeman.

"A gun?" Rocky was amazed. "What yer mean – a gun?"

Pale-faced, Pa Richardson's nephew replied, "No – was another boy – taller, an' he had a cowboy hat on. He was standin' just next ter this one."

Rocky observed that the policeman was beginning to have some doubts, and when he was asked about the boy with the gun he looked him straight in the eyes. "Was nobody like dat around," he said. "Yer wuddent have somebody wid a cowboy hat an' a gun in Larkspur Lane, *wud* yer?" He winked and put a finger to his forehead, looking sideways at Pa Richardson's nephew in a knowing way. "Look, mister, I'm goin' ter be late for school if you don't let me geroff!"

"What's yer name?"

"Rocky. Rocky O'Rourke. Dey know me at Larkspur Lane. Ask McMahon. Dey owe me."

The policeman obviously didn't believe this. "Yer can go," he said.

"Ta very much," said Rocky and, to Pa Richardson's nephew, "Hope yer get over it. Dey can treat that sort of thing now, the doctors."

And he went out, triumphant.

"Hi, wacks!" he greeted the rest of the gang, who had arrived and had been watching what was going on.

"They arrested you for somethin', Rocky?" asked Billy anxiously.

"No. Was the Nabber. He's got the Colt and Pa Richardson's nephew thought it was a hold-up. The Nabber run off!"

"With his hat? An' his gun?" asked Beady.

"Dat's right. Was a good gun, but," said Rocky. "One of dem that doesn't work," and they fell about laughing.

But as they started along Larkspur Lane, Billy asked, "Yer don't think the police'll get on to the Nabber?"

"No chance. I indicated to them that Pa Richardson's nephew could be a lead head. Anyway, it's put

82

the Nabber off life, an' we're both saggin'. Youse comin'?"

But Beady, Billy and Little Chan couldn't see any percentage in sagging. They'd just get battered. It was different for Rocky, because his mother never took any interest in where he was, and the Nabber's mother, from what they heard, seemed to think he was the kind of statue you could find in churches.

As they got to the school gates, the tall black boy on skates and wearing a woollen hat that Rocky had seen before swirled round them. "Things is boilin' up," he said. "Watch it. Trouble soon." And he skated away.

"What's he on about?" asked Beady.

"Just a nutter," said Rocky. "There's a lot of dem round here, apart from the Nabber. Yer not saggin'? Well, enjoy yerselves. Der's more life in me brother Joey!" and giving them up, he started off along the Boulevard.

They were all right, the Cats, he thought as he ran, for things like football and hanging about, but when you were into something really exciting and profitable, you could only rely on the Nabber, and he wouldn't go too far, neither, he reflected. And he started to think of the things he really needed that he might be able to nick on a visit downtown.

The Nabber was at the bus stop without hat or gun, hunched in his camouflage jacket, dejected at the end of a queue of senior citizens.

"Cheer up, wack!" Rocky greeted him. "We'll get some good loot. . ."

"Yer not bringin' *her*?"

83

It was Suzie, following him. "Saggin', Rocky," she said.

"Yer not saggin' – get back ter de school!"

"Saggin'," said Suzie, frowning stubbornly.

The Nabber turned away, disgusted. "Goin' down town wid a tiddler – why don't yer just run a nursery?"

"I'll *do* you, Nabber! An' Suzie – back ter school, or me mam'll batter yer! Yer know she will!"

"You swine!" exclaimed Suzie, but unfortunately at that moment the bus drew up, and with a last, "Go away, Suzie," from Rocky, he and the Nabber got on.

"Now then, boys," said the bus driver, who happened to be Beady Martin's uncle, as Rocky and the Nabber tried to get on unnoticed among the senior citizens with their passes, "you have to pay some money. Wouldn't like to see you leavin' the bus with a guilty conscience. And is this small girl with you?"

Suzie was scrambling in behind them. "Can't stop her, Nabber," said Rocky apologetically. "She'll not be any bother."

The Nabber was sarcastic. "Heard it all before," he said and, to the driver, "he's a child-minder."

"Put a trap on yer moey, Nabber, or I'll put yer eye in a sling!"

"You two remind me of the United Nations," said Beady's uncle, "but I have a schedule to keep to. Would it put you out to settle things about that child?"

"She's my sister – she gets on free," retorted Rocky.

"Don't believe him," said the Nabber, beginning to feel better. "S'not his sister. It's a limpet he picked up on New Brighton sands."

"I can't understand," said Beady's uncle thoughtfully, "how it is that you are here when you should be where Beady is."

"He could clat on us," said the Nabber, as they dropped into seats upstairs in the bus.

"He wuddent clat – Beady's uncle wuddent."

They reflected on life for a few minutes, then the Nabber said, "We'll go ter the arcade first an' have a go at the machines."

"Yer got the money?"

"Got *some*."

"Right. An' are yer feelin' the cold without yer hat?"

"Do you!"

And they had a minor punch-up, which indicated that the Nabber was coming out of shock.

"What we doin' den?" asked the Nabber as they got off the bus.

"Just messin' about. Hi, we'll be lushes, out of the pub, havin' a fight. Come on, walk like a rubber-legs!"

So they walked like rubber-legs, swaying about the pavement, shouting at each other, with Suzie following, fascinated. As they measured unsteadily up to each other, some people avoided them and some stopped to watch.

"Disgustin'," the crowd said. "How old are dey?"

"Get in der, lads!" shouted a supporter.

85

"Here's a judy comin'," somebody else shouted, and everybody returned to their own business, including Rocky, the Nabber and Suzie, so that the WPC had nothing to get a grip on, though she followed them as far as Lime Street Station, when her radio started crackling and she lost interest.

They went into the games arcade near St John's Precinct, and Rocky gave Suzie a ten-pence piece to have a go on the Space Shuttle while he and Nabber tried out the Space Invaders. But Suzie went to stand beside one of the fruit machines, watching a man put in coin after coin, getting nothing back. When he gave up and walked away, she put in the ten-pence piece and pressed the buttons: the money flowed out. Suzie was ecstatic, until the man came back, pushed her aside and started scooping up the money. It was then that Suzie swore at him and shouted for Rocky, which brought the Nabber as well, and the man in charge of the arcade.

"What's it, Suzie?" asked Rocky.

"Put it in – ten pence. *My* money," spluttered Suzie.

"The ten pence I give yer?"

Suzie nodded furiously.

"Yer heard her," said Rocky to the man in charge.

"Was *my* money before dat, but," said the other man. "Anyway, she's too young for dis."

"Wasn't *her* ten pence but," said Rocky. "Was *his*," indicating the Nabber, who looked old enough to carry some weight in the discussion.

"*She* put the money in, but," said the man.

"On *his* account," said Rocky firmly.

86

"Dat's right," said the Nabber, virtuously.

To restore peace, the man in charge awarded half the money to the Nabber and half to the other man.

"It's a rip-off!" shouted Rocky.

"It's my decision. And get out, all of youse, and don't come back!"

They ran up Church Street towards Lewis's store, their pockets heavy with coins, Suzie shouting incoherently behind them. In the shop they stopped, laughing and panting.

"Yer have ter hand it to her," gasped the Nabber, "she's worth takin' around."

"Told yer!"

"Loot," Suzie demanded, so Rocky gave her some, and she shot off into the store.

"Have ter go after her," said Rocky.

"What for, but?" asked the Nabber. "She doesn't self-destruct."

They found her in the Grotto among the lights and toadstools, goblins and a fairy queen, but Suzie had planted herself in front of Santa Claus in her worn jeans and anorak and tattered bow of ribbon, and with fierce eyes.

Santa Claus bent towards her. "Hello, little girl," he said in his 'ho-ho' voice (though if it had been the rush hour he would probably have ignored her). "And what's *your* name?"

Suzie frowned and told him.

"Well, Suzie, wur's yer mam?"

Suzie's frown turned to a scowl, and Santa Claus cast a 'rescue me' look at the fairy queen, who didn't notice because, since business was slack, she was sitting on a toadstool examining her polished fingernails.

"Well," Santa Claus pressed on, "and what would *you* like for Christmas?"

"A new mam!" Suzie shouted. "Want a new mam!"

"Ho-ho," chortled Santa Claus, uneasily. "You can't mean that, little girl. I'm sure you have a very good—"

"New mam!"

At this point Rocky grabbed her and urged her to "Shurrup!"

"What's up wid her?" asked Santa Claus, forgetting his 'ho-ho' voice. "Somethin' upset her?"

"Just a bit excited like," replied Rocky. "If yer give her her present, it'll be all right."

"But she said she wanted. . ."

"Forget it – give her the present – the one she's due for."

Santa Claus recovered and began, "Well now, little girl, and what's your. . ."

"Listen, mister," said Rocky desperately, because Suzie had picked up a cardboard stone from the floor of the Grotto and was preparing to launch it, "just give her a present – any present!"

Santa Claus hastily handed Suzie a box done up in pink paper, and Rocky pulled Suzie out of the Grotto as she stripped the parcel of its wrappings and produced a small red plastic shoulder bag with a blue dolphin on the front.

"Well, dat's nice, Suzie, in't it?" he said encouragingly, since Suzie looked as though she was going to rip it apart as well. "Could keep yer money in it."

Suzie thought about this, grinned, opened the bag and pulled out a red brush and comb and a small mirror. She looked at herself in that and shouted, "Me, Rocky! Me!"

"Dat's right, Suzie. Now put it all back wid yer money. . ."

"Are we doin' some robbin' or are yer takin' up bein' a nanny full-time?" asked the Nabber, who was fed up with hanging about.

So Rocky got some batteries for Joey's torch, as he knew he was going to need it in working order, and a pair of gloves which he knew he would also need, and the Nabber got a scarf which he thought would go with the hat if he ever dared wear it again, and Suzie picked up one or two things.

Then the Nabber muttered to Rocky, "This place is crawlin' with store 'tecs."

"How d'yer know?"

"A woman der's been fingerin' a woolly hat for hours an' the judy behind the counter's not bothered."

"Come on, den," said Rocky. "We'll clear off."

But the woman was suddenly beside them, saying, "Just a moment. . ."

They didn't wait. They were out of the shop in two seconds flat and up Hardman Street and on to the top deck of a bus in another four, where they subsided, panting, and considered things.

"Best thing about that trip was de fruit machine," the Nabber reflected.

"Got a idea, Nabber. 'Bout that house."

"What's it?"

"Just workin' it out."

"Think yer might get it done by dis time next year?" The Nabber was sarcastic.

"Listen, lead head, der's better things in dat house than in Lewis's, an' I don't *need* yer around! Can do it meself!" And Rocky pushed his hand furiously through his red hair. "Had enough of you, Nabber. Yer could start a row in a empty house!"

The Nabber shrugged. "Just dat I know your ideas never work out."

"Well, I have dem, anyway. More than *you* can say!"

"Do youse two know anything about a little girl downstairs?" asked the conductor, who had made a special trip up to ask this question.

"Suzie!" Rocky exclaimed, having forgotten all about her. "It'll be me sister! She all right?"

"Depends," said the conductor, "what yer mean by 'right'. But don't forget to take her with you. Don't think Lost Property would accept her."

Suzie was sitting in the front seat of the bus, looking out of the window.

"Tatty-'ead!" Rocky exclaimed. "What yer up to?"

Suzie turned to him.

"Don't believe it," muttered Rocky.

"Warped herself, hasn't she?" said the Nabber. "Who's she now? Boy George?"

★

90

"Yer'll have ter scrub the lipstick off an' get de earrings off," Rocky insisted, as they got to St Catherine's Square. "Me mam'll go spare if she sees dem. Yer know dat, Suzie. An' we've had enough trouble wid her."

For a few moments Suzie glared stubbornly at him, then she relented, unclipped the red plastic earrings and rubbed furiously at her mouth with the sleeve of her anorak, which didn't really help matters, Rocky thought. Then she put the earrings in her handbag.

"Der's lipstick in der?"

Suzie nodded.

"Don't know whether yer should even let her see the bag," Rocky said, worried.

Suzie looked up at him, and then at the trodden patch of garden. "Dead," she suggested. "bury." She had once buried a Barbie doll there, which she had decided was dead.

"S'all right, tatty-'ead. Keep it. Only don't let her see the earrings an' lipstick. Put *dem* in yer pocket for the time bein'."

Very seriously, Suzie took these items from the bag and put them in her pocket. "Right, Rocky?" she asked.

"Right. An' keep quiet an' let me do all der talkin', an' don't start yellin' whatever happens. Got it?"

Suzie nodded furiously.

Then he thought of something else. "Wur's de money yer won?"

"Purse."

"Well, all right, but don't wave it about."

91

He looked cautiously into the living room of Number 3. It was all right, because Mrs Flanagan was asleep in her chair in front of the electric fire, her feet on the stool, one of her paper-backed romances on her knee and the telly on. She did not stir as Rocky pulled Suzie in, sat her down on the settee, extracted a pizza from a paper bag on the table and shared it with Suzie. They ate in silence, with an eye on Mrs Flanagan. The old alarm clock on the mantelpiece that was hiccuping time away with an occasional protesting whirr said that it was half past eight. Of course, that was just guesswork on its part, but it would be near enough.

"Got ter go out, Suzie," Rocky whispered. "Be all right?"

Suzie gave a quick look at Mrs Flanagan. "Go wid you."

"Yer can't. Not be long. Yer could go inter Joey's bed."

When Suzie had curled up under the blankets, Rocky cautiously opened the window and dropped out into the alley behind the house, closing the window, all but, behind him. Then he pulled up his collar, pushed his hands into his pockets and started silently for the Ratman's house.

He flattened himself against the wall beside a telegraph pole near the back door, and waited. It was quiet. Nothing happened. He was just thinking of giving up, when he heard a key turn in a lock, and the door opened. He tried to make himself flat as a slice of toast, and held his breath. He could hear the Ratman muttering, the door closing and being locked.

"There's ways and means," said the Ratman. Rocky went cold, thinking he must have been seen, but the Ratman's footsteps went along the alley towards Crown Street, and when Rocky looked round the telegraph pole he could see the long, oblong figure, like a walking coffin, Rocky thought, going on towards St Catherine's Square.

He made for the Steps down to Larkspur Lane and then on to the streets near the Cathedral, narrow streets of small terraced houses, his hair silver in the lamplight. He didn't do anything, just walked and muttered and then went back home. Rocky watched him go into the yard, and heard the lock being turned. And that was all.

He's a right nutter, Rocky thought, as he climbed back through the window at Number 3 and got into bed where he lay thinking about the situation. One night's sussing wasn't enough. Have to go out again tomorrow.

CHAPTER

6

Each night, Rocky went to the alley behind the Ratman's house about nine o'clock and, in the shadows and huddled in his anorak, he waited and watched the back door. And each night the old man came out of the back door, locked it and started off. It was a weird business following him. Sometimes he went in one direction and sometimes in another. But always eventually he made for the streets behind the Cathedral. Once he was attacked by an alsatian dog, whose owner just managed to pull the dog off before it did some damage. But that didn't seem to upset the Ratman. He just muttered to himself, "There's dogs and dogs, and cats and cats," and walked on. He muttered to himself a lot.

Rocky couldn't see that there was any point in these walks, except for the exercise, but they always started at nine and ended at ten o'clock. But on the third night, the Ratman went to a small shop in a terrace behind the Cathedral. The shop was dark, but he tapped at the door. It was opened and he went in. About half an hour later, he came out, carrying a plastic bag of what looked like groceries, and the pockets of his coat looked a bit bulkier. Funny way to do your shopping, Rocky thought, tracking him back and jumping out of sight into a doorway at one point when the old man suddenly looked round as though he suspected he was being followed, though he didn't seem to have seen Rocky. But he did say, pointing to his nose, "There's nose and knows," before he went back to his house, went in through the back door and locked it behind him.

Not getting far, Rocky thought as he ran home. He couldn't keep it up much longer, and all he'd found out was that the time to get into the house was between nine and ten. But how did he get in, when it was always locked? If he couldn't think up a plan, the Nabber would really welly him and get the Cats on *his* side, and then Joey would do it – certain to.

In Number 3 there was an unusual silence. The telly wasn't going, Suzie was asleep in bed and his mother was sitting in her chair, staring at the electric fire. She didn't even turn round as he came in.

"Wur've yer been?" she asked in a dull voice.

"Just out, yer know like. Cold enough for two pair of boot-laces, in't it?" he said, trying to take her mind off where he'd been.

"Yer always out. What yer up to?" But she didn't sound really interested. It wasn't like his mam not to have a row if she didn't get an explanation.

"Yer all right?" he asked. "Yer want der telly on?"

She didn't reply straight away, then she turned to him, and he could see she'd been crying. That wasn't like his mam, either.

"If things go on like this, der'll be no telly ter put on," she said tragically.

"What for, but? What's the matter?" It sounded like the end of the world, having no telly.

"Nothin' from Flanagan. If he doesn't come back. . ."

"He'll come back, mam. He'll have to. He'll come for Suzie, anyway, won't he?"

"Yer never can tell." And Mrs Flanagan subsided into gloom again.

Rocky considered things. It *would* be the end if Flanagan didn't come back — be the end for Suzie, anyway. On the other hand, if he could get some loot out of that house. . .

"Hi," he said, trying to be cheerful, "we'll have the telly on while we've got it, and I'll make a cuppa."

"Yer not a bad lad," his mother conceded, as she drank her tea. "But yer don't know what I have ter put up with." Then she sighed and cheered up a bit. "Well," she said, "der's always the social security, in't there?"

Watching the Cats' team warming up in Princes Park next morning, in a variety of tee-shirts ranging in colour from puce to orange, Billy thought they weren't showing a lot of interest in the match with the Allsorts. This wasn't surprising, since they hadn't had a good practice for weeks, and Rocky wasn't doing much except wandering around the pitch and occasionally kicking the ball. It worried Billy, because he had the impression that the Allsorts were a well co-ordinated team, and he didn't want to see the Cats trodden into the ground.

Mr Oliver arrived and assessed the situation. "Yer haven't forgot again, have yer, Rocky? Wur's the opposin' team?"

"No, Mr Oliver. Billy's got it all arranged, haven't yer, Billy? Dey should be here any minit." But his mind was on getting into the Ratman's house. He yawned.

"Are yer with us, Rocky?" demanded the wingy. "Yer look half asleep. Yer need a couple of match-sticks ter prop yer eyes open with? What yer been up to?"

"S'all right, Mr Oliver." Rocky tried to look wide awake. "S'all right."

"Think that's the Allsorts," said Billy.

"An' all their friends and relatives," muttered the Nabber.

A crowd was running through the park gates towards them – at least it seemed like a crowd – and the Cats came together behind Mr Oliver, watching. The Allsorts were all colours, and they were all dressed in black, with a skull and cross-bones drawn in luminous paint on their tee-shirts. Their supporters – and there were many of them – had a skull and cross-bones painted on them wherever there was a space suitable for decorating.

The Allsorts immediately started running on the spot and doing exercises, and a tall black boy with dreadlocks under a red woolly hat and balancing on skates came up to Rocky and said he was their captain and let's get started. It was Nelson, the one who had looked at him through a rolled-up newspaper outside school. He was still wearing skates, and didn't appear to be going to take them off.

Trouble coming, all right, thought Rocky, but he said, trying to seem to be in charge but worried because the Cats had no supporters except Billy and Suzie, "Right, we'll get the goal posts marked. An' I've got the ball, an' supporters keep well off the pitch. Right?"

"Right. An' I'm Howard."

"An' I'm Rocky. Is the trouble still comin'?"

"Still comin'," said Howard very seriously. "An' who's that man?"

"Mr Oliver. He's the ref."

Howard looked suspiciously at Mr Oliver. "How's he the ref? Only got one—"

"He used ter play for Liverpool," Rocky cut in. "That's why he's the ref."

Howard considered the matter. "All right. He's der ref," he concluded. "We toss for kick-off." And then confidentially he asked Rocky, "Who's takin' der bets? I got a friend here. . ."

"Billy'll do that. But we have just der one bet, see? Both the teams put in a pound, and the winner gets both."

Howard shrugged. "All right for this time. But we generally do more than that. Anyhow, we all have bets among ourselves, an' you're free to put any on yer want."

"Rocky," said Billy, as Howard went off, "I don't like this."

"Yer right not to, skin," replied Rocky. "But don't worry. We'll do dem. Hi, Cats!" and the Cats' team came round him. "This lot's dangerous," Rocky said. "Yer'll have ter watch them. And don't let their supporters get yer down, see? Don't listen to them. Just concentrate on der game."

"All very well," said the Nabber laconically, but with a rather worried look, "but if dey lose, their supporters could run wild."

"Dey won't," said Rocky. "I'll see about it."

At the centre of the pitch, Howard, Rocky and the wingy consulted.

"There's this thing," said Rocky. "If you lose, we don't want your lot comin' at us. Yer know like?"

"They won't. We'll win, but." Howard was certain, and still had his skates on.

"That's ter be seen," said the wingy. "But if you've got that many supporters, yer have ter be able ter control them. Can you?"

"They might fight among themselves," said Howard, "but only if some have put bets on the Cats and the Cats lose."

"There'll be no bets," said the wingy.

Howard shrugged. "How can you stop them?"

"Where's yer goal posts?" asked Rocky.

"Where's yours?"

"Those two anoraks."

"Ours is those two boys." Howard pointed to two boys standing at attention at the other end of the

99

pitch, the regulation distance apart. "They are always our goal posts."

"Your team played a lot of matches?" the wingy asked, suspiciously.

"Lots. Generally win."

Rocky rubbed his hand through his red hair. "Never seen a set-up like this," he muttered.

"Right. We'll get started," said the wingy. "And I'll be keepin' a eye on yer goal posts." Which was just as well, because when, after a quarter of an hour's play, Little Chan sent the ball to Rocky and Rocky sent it towards the Allsorts' goal, one goal post moved swiftly inwards, so that the ball went wide.

The wingy blew his whistle. "Right," he said to Howard. "That's a goal for the Cats. And it will be, every time a goal post moves, in whatever direction. That understood?"

Howard smiled sheepishly. "All right. I'll pass the word," he said.

Meanwhile the Allsorts' supporters were yelling their heads off, jumping up and down and break-dancing. It was nerve-racking for the Cats. Their only supporter was Suzie, who never knew who she was shouting for.

Rocky got them together. "Listen," he said. "Yer'l have ter ignore them. Concentrate on de game."

"They're fierce, but," objected Beady.

"And very noisy," added Little Chan.

"Look, we're goin' ter beat them," said Rocky "Yer can welly them if yer like. Yer have my permission."

100

After that, following Rocky's advice, the Cats threw themselves into the game, ignoring the Allsorts' supporters. Beady blocked an Allsorts' try and got the ball out to Little Chan, who dribbled it round Howard and got it to Beady, who lifted it over to the Nabber, who messed around a bit but eventually got it to Rocky, and since the goal posts were no longer mobile, he scored.

But it didn't help. The Cats were no match for the Allsorts, who seemed to be everywhere at once, always passed the ball right and frequently got it into the Cats' goal. The Cats flagged, and Rocky knew they were flagging. He was flagging himself – he just hadn't got the energy to do anything about it after those nights following the Ratman around.

The wingy couldn't do anything about it either. Rocky heard him saying things like, "Got yer boots buttered? Wur's yer sense of direction? Whose side yer playin' on? Why don't youse all go an' have a nice rest?" And eventually, overcome, he shouted at Rocky, who had been taking the ball towards the Allsorts' goal and then been intercepted by Howard, who took it successfully in the other direction, "Why don't yer *do* somethin'? Pull his leg off and hit him wid he soggy end!"

Then, recovering himself, he blew the whistle and went to shake hands with Howard and congratulate he Allsorts. Unhappily, Rocky did likewise, and Billy went to pay over the pound the Cats had had on the game.

"Return match when yer like," said Howard, fastening on his skates. "Any time."

"Thanks very much," replied Rocky, without any enthusiasm.

Rubbing himself down with a towel and watching with definite relief as the Allsorts streamed towards the park gates, singing, the Nabber declared, "Not facin' that lot again. That's it. An' I can think of better things ter do on a Saturday mornin'."

"We'll get some practice in – get some new players."

From underneath the sweater the Nabber was pulling over his head a voice mumbled a message which became clearer as the Nabber's head emerged, and which Rocky interpreted as, "An' dey'll want a return game an' bring all that lot with them – no way. I'm resigning."

"Have ter get some supporters, Rocky," said Billy.

"Wur from, but?"

"Put an addy in der *Echo*," suggested the Nabber. "'Supporters wanted for team on its last legs.' Great!"

"An' who scored an own goal?"

"An' who never got within two spitting distances of the Allsorts' goal?"

"Now then, wacks," said the wingy, who was looking a bit brighter. "Don't wear yerselves out. Was a good match."

The Nabber groaned. "Yer have ter be jokin'."

"No. Dey're a good team, and youse didn't do too badly, considerin' yer never seem ter get any practice in. Yer'll do better next time, or my name's not Dave Oliver. But I'll have ter put yer through it. Practice here next Saturday. Right?"

"We'll never beat them, but," said Rocky.

"We will, but it'll be painful," the wingy assured him. "You got nothin' else ter say to yer team?"

Rocky thought desperately, then he shouted, "What's wrong wid youse lot? Think it was a funeral! Come on! The Pool forever!" and he started running towards the park gates. The Cats team followed, shouting – even the wingy was shouting, and Suzie was shouting, "Wait, Rocky! Too fast!"

"Here, lads," said the wingy, when they got to Mrs Aber's house, "all me small change. Go an' drown yer sorrows!" He brought a fistful of coins out of his pocket.

The Nabber stepped forward immediately to take them, but Rocky nudged him back. Wasn't fair on Mr Oliver.

"Der's no need," he said, "an' it would buy yer a pint, that lot."

The wingy considered. "Yer right, Rocky, an' I could do wid one after all that runnin' around, but I'm self-sacrificin', see? An' what's more" – with a wink – "I've got a quid or two the wife doesn't know about. So go on an' have a Coke on me, all on youse. An' I'll see yer next Saturday."

"How much is it?" asked the Nabber as they walked on.

Rocky counted the money. "Der's one twenty."

"Big deal!" said the Nabber. "Twenty-five pence each!"

"Less if yer count Suzie in," said Billy.

"Who's countin' *her* in?" asked the Nabber.

"S'better than nothin'," Rocky concluded. "Come on!"

"You won't have to buy *me* Coke," said Little Chan, as they went down the Steps to Larkspur Lane. "I have to go home."

They got the Cokes from the newsagents, since Pa Richardson's was closed, and as they leant on the wires across his window the late September sun dazzled and warmed them. They talked in a relaxed way of how they would defeat the Allsorts next time, and how they could get some supporters.

"Der's the tiddlers in Joseph Terrace," said Rocky. "They'll do anything for a few five-pence pieces."

"Better have a proper bet next time," said the Nabber. "Could have made a bomb today."

"*If* yer'd bet on the Allsorts," said Billy.

"Couldn't do that," said Beady.

"Why not, but?" And the Nabber kicked an empty can across the road. "Yer have ter bet on the winners!" Then he added quickly, "Watch it – scuffers!"

The Cats remained casual as Constable McMahon approached them.

"What yer hangin' round here for?" he asked.

"We're not doin' nothin'," Rocky retorted. "Just been playin' footy and come down for a Coke. And we paid for dem! Mr Oliver give us the money – yer can ask him!"

"Right. But don't be here too long. I'll be back."

As he walked away, the Cats erupted into silent derision, making faces and vulgar gestures until the constable reached the Steps and turned round to find the Cats silent and casually contemplating Chan's chippy opposite.

Then the Nabber yawned. "This has ter be the most boring day of my life!" he said. "An' you're supposed ter be the entertainments manager – what yer got lined up? Got yer plan for gettin' into that house yet? Goin' ter use a tin-opener? Or have yer given up?"

"I'm not tellin' *my* plans to a mate who's too scared to go inter the place!"

"I'm not scared ter go in – dat's nothin', but I never said I *could* get in – not like the one that jumps up an' never comes down!"

Rocky was furious. "I'll chin yer, Nabber, for that!" He stalked away towards the Steps, where he turned and shouted, "I'll show youse! All on youse! An' yer'll get none of the loot!"

It was a dramatic outburst, and the Cats were rather stunned.

"I didn't say nothin'," muttered Beady, puzzled. "Didn't say nothin'."

"Bag of gas!" retorted the Nabber.

Billy said nothing, but he pulled his scarf tighter round his neck and thought to himself that Rocky was worried and maybe afraid – but he would never admit to it.

"Have to gerron," he said. "See youse," and he pedalled away towards St Catherine's Buildings.

By four o'clock, Rocky couldn't stand the suspense of waiting any longer. Nothing could take his mind

105

off what he had to do, not the television, not even the Doomlord and Enok. He went over to look out of the window on to the empty Square, kicking his foot against the skirting-board, wishing he hadn't boasted to the Cats and thinking they should be going with him anyway – but they were all cowards!

"Will yer stop that!" his mother shouted, angry that her Saturday afternoon television trance was being disturbed. "Yer'll have a hole in it! If you can't stay still, get yerself out!"

So Rocky took her advice and did. As he stood in the deserted Square, he had an idea. After all, he had what was left of the American's two pounds. He started running, but stopped on the corner when he saw the wingy talking to McMahon. They hadn't seen him, so he ran back through the courtyard of St Catherine's Buildings, up Joseph Terrace (you could always get through there safely, if you ran quick enough), on to Princes Boulevard and into the Baptist Church Hall. It was time he joined the Youth Club again, if he was going to get to their Christmas party, which was the only reason he ever joined.

In the Baptist Hall, Betty Malloney had the tea mugs lined up on the table like ranks of guards, with a bowl of sugar and jug of milk at each end, and she was just about to make the tea when Rocky appeared, breathless and not very respectable-looking, but with the air of knowing where he was and what he could get.

"Hello dur, Betty," he greeted her amicably. "How's things?"

"What yer want?" she asked, stolidly making tea.

106

"Want ter join again. Got me subs."

"Yer can't join. Yer too much trouble."

"I'm not any trouble! What've I done?"

"Yer know as well as I do. When you left last Christmas, der was two invitations for the Old People's Christmas Tea missing from the desk in Mr Fernhead's office. And you was the last in there. Yer can clear off, 'cos we know yer!" and Betty turned away.

Rocky looked round the hall, thinking. The pop-mobility and the darts and the table tennis were going on. It was a mass of activity – useless as far as Rocky was concerned. A notice on the board advertised a disco next week.

"Wur's he? Mr Fernhead?" he asked, always believing in getting to the top man if he could.

"He's left."

"Left? What dey always leavin' for? Dat's two of dem I've gone through. Means yer have ter start again every time."

"It's Mr Hunt now. An' yer can't go inter his office. . ." but Rocky had already gone.

The office was a lot tidier than it had been when Mr Fernhead had been there, and a bald-headed man sitting at the desk looked disconcertingly at Rocky through a pair of gold-rimmed granny glasses.

"Yes?" he said.

"'Lo der," said Rocky amicably. "Want ter join der club. Got der money for subs."

"Mr Hunt," – it was Betty Malloney behind him – "this is Rocky O'Rourke. He always joins this time of

107

the year for the Christmas party, an' he always gets in fights, and Mr Fernhead said he couldn't come back because last year he *stole* two tickets for the Old People's Christmas Tea from *that* desk!" She pointed, indignant and virtuous, to the desk.

"S'not true!" Rocky was angry, but he put on an air of outraged innocence. "Didn't pinch dem tickets. I was due for dem. I'd paid me subs. I was due for dem! An' I gave dem ter old people – *an'* I didn't get no Christmas party – haven't had one *yet*! *An'* I join about dis time 'cos the nights is dark an' me mam's always out an' I can't get inter the house. Have ter go somewhere. *An'* I've saved up for me subs. Look – got a quid. Yer can't stop me from joinin'. *An'* I don't wear out your table tennis tables or yer darts board or yer floor much! *An'* yer can't believe *her* – she's always been against me *and* me mam, and. . ."

He had come to the end of inspiration, and paused to assess the effect. There was no effect on Mr Hunt, who continued to look at him through the granny glasses. It put Rocky off, because he looked like a rent-feller, or the one that paid out the family allowances at the post office. Him with the bike on his nose, Rocky thought fiercely, while looking dishevelled but appealing.

"His family is well-known in the Square as being the *worst*," contributed Betty Malloney.

Rocky turned, smiling, towards her and muttered, "Do yer fer that!"

"Well." Mr Hunt had become judicious. "The rules have changed slightly, Rocky, since you were last here, which would be – one year ago? And now you'll have your membership card dated by me each time you come, and a comment on behaviour added. Right?"

Rocky considered whether it was worth it. "Yer havin' a Christmas party?"

"We might be having a pantomime." He had taken a membership card from a neat pile and his pen was poised above it, as he looked over his spectacles at Rocky.

"But yer'll have cakes and presents?"

Mr Hunt shrugged. "Maybe. It's a risk you have to take."

It was worth risking fifty pence, Rocky decided, and got his membership card. "Thanks very much. I'll have me tea and biscuit now."

Betty Malloney poured his tea reluctantly, but that didn't worry him. He wandered about the room, watching the popmobility and the darts and the table tennis, and helped himself to another biscuit when Betty Malloney wasn't looking. Then he went back to the office and, smiling, put his card down in front of Mr Hunt.

"Have ter go now, mister," he said. "So can yer write yer comment?"

Mr Hunt looked at him suspiciously.

"You haven't been here long," he said.

"Can't stay long this time. Me mam's not well, see. Have ter get back. Stay longer next week."

Mr Hunt's pen hovered reluctantly over Rocky's membership card, which already had a tea-stained, creased appearance.

"And what is your special interest?"

109

"What yer mean?" Rocky was genuinely puzzled, and a bit suspicious. What had *his* special interest to do with this feller, he wondered, and prepared to take him up on it.

"What have you done while you've been here this afternoon?"

"What yer think? Had me tea an' biscuit."

"But what else? Have you taken part in any activity?" Mr Hunt was persistent behind his granny glasses.

"What yer on about?" Rocky demanded, and then it dawned on him, and he said with a conciliatory smile, "Well, yer know like, der's a lot goin' on, so I was just sort of sussin' – well, watchin' and tryin' ter make me mind up for next time."

"So what will you join in?"

Rocky thought desperately. "Darts."

"Darts. Very well." And there was nothing Mr Hunt could do but write on Rocky's card, "Behaviour good. Interest darts."

So having got that in writing, on the way out Rocky tripped up a table-tennis player, had a verbal encounter with a darts player and disrupted the popmobility by staggering though their ranks like a lush. It had all been very satisfactory, and he was on his way to the Christmas party, or pantomime or whatever. He raced along the Boulevard, triumphant, until the growing darkness transformed it into Ratman country, and he began to think he might just stay in bed that night. He could always tell the Cats he hadn't been able to get into that house – but he knew how much mileage the Nabber would make out of that!

CHAPTER
7

It happened that night. Rocky heard the door being opened, and the old man come out, and the door shut behind him. He walked away, but one sound was missing: he hadn't locked the door. Rocky couldn't believe it – it was luck! But was it? Had the Ratman just forgotten to lock the door, or was it deliberate? A trap? Thinking of the way he'd thrown the ball back over the wall, Rocky could believe it was a trap. But the old man had cleared off, wasn't in sight, so he decided to risk it and cautiously pushed open the door, went into the yard and waited again, listening. Then he switched on Joey's torch, which was useful as a weapon as well as a source of light, pulled on the gloves he'd nicked from Lewis's and crossed the yard to the back door of the house. Again he paused, listening, then he tried the door. It wasn't locked, either. It was definitely a trap, but he wanted to see inside that house. There was no sound of anybody about, only the traffic on Princes Boulevard, so he pushed the door open.

From the darkness came a smell of dirt and rotting meat. It made him feel sick, but he shone the torch and went inside, closing the door behind him. He was in a big kitchen with an old-fashioned sink, like the one in the hideout, with a tap dripping into it. It was very cold and silent, except for some creakings and squeakings. There was only a narrow passage through the kitchen, because on each side there were stacks of pie and cake containers, some of them Mr Kipling's, and some with nibbled cakes and pies falling out, and cartons of apple juice, some of which were empty and some had been nibbled and the juice had dripped on to the floor. Up above, the cobwebs formed a second ceiling, and shoals of black beetles swarmed away from the torchlight.

Better nick something quick and get out, he thought, and started through the kitchen, his feet sinking into what felt like soil but was probably layers of dirt. Then he stepped on to something soft and yielding, and leapt back. The torchlight showed that it was a dead rat, its fur grey and glossy, and he remembered the rat that had run out of the house. He decided then that he wasn't going on – all the loot in the world wouldn't make it worthwhile, not with the dirt, the darkness, the creakings and squeakings. The nutter was a Ratman all right.

But as he turned back to the door, it opened, the light was switched on and the old man was there, his face thin as a hatchet under the light. He loomed above Rocky, saying nothing.

Straight away, Rocky tried to dodge past him to the door, but it was slammed and locked.

"There's caught and court," the old man chanted triumphantly. "When yer caught, yer go to court. Trapped yer, didn't I?"

Rocky thought fast. He had to get out of this.

"What yer on about, mister?" he asked indignantly, but beginning to shake. "Was helpin' yer out. Was just comin' through de alley on me way home an' saw de door open, so I come in – could have been a murder. . ."

He looked like an eagle, the old man, with his sharp nose and deepset eyes, and he gave a laugh which sounded like a squawk. "With yer gloves and yer torch?" he asked.

"Me brother's torch – lends it to me when I'm out in the dark. . ."

"And why are you out in the dark?"

"Because. . ." But Rocky couldn't think of anything. He *was* trapped like a rat, and if that old man got the police and he was taken to court and sent away, what would that do his mam? – and Flanagan? – and Suzie?

"Listen, mister," he said desperately. "I haven't done nothin'! I haven't took nothin'! Told yer, I was just. . ."

"Followin' me, looking through windows and over walls, kicking a football into the yard. So the doors were left open, and I saw you come in, and" – he clapped his hands together as if he'd caught a fly – "I got yer!"

He pushed past Rocky, his head knocking against the ceiling light, which swayed so that the shadows swayed and made the man seem even taller. He kicked the dead rat out of his way and said, "Come on."

Reluctantly, Rocky followed him into a passage narrowed by piles of books and papers. Doing the bin men

113

out of their job, he thought. The man opened a door and switched on the light with the air of a magician, and they were looking at the back of the statue Rocky had seen. Another door was opened and another light switched on, and a fortune in silver and china and furniture appeared among the cobwebs.

"A lifetime," the man muttered. "A lifetime. A lifetime's fortune. Everything must be kept, collected, stored. Everything. No waste."

Rocky was sure then that he was locked up with a madman. It was Dragons and Dungeons all right.

The man went into another room, small, with a table, a couple of easy chairs, a desk with a telephone on it, a pair of brass scales and a black notebook. Rocky stood in the doorway.

The man picked up the receiver. "I'll get the police," he said.

"No, don't, mister — listen, I haven't took nothin'. . ." Rocky was sweating in spite of the cold.

"I stopped you."

"Wasn't goin' to, but. Not a thief. Yer can ask them down at Larkspur Lane — dey know me. I caught a terrorist for them — they owe me!"

The old man sat down in one of the chairs in a way that suggested he spent a lot of time in it. "There's caught and court," he muttered, and then went into a silence.

"Yer never feel de cold, mister?" asked Rocky, shivering with cold and apprehension. "Yer never get pneumonia in here?"

The man didn't seem to hear him. Could be

here for life, Rocky thought, imagining some small windowless room upstairs, cold and rat-infested and locked, where he could starve or freeze to death.

"Out of the trap," the old man said, as though he hadn't heard him. "Out of the trap. Conditions. You take certain things to certain places for me – at certain times."

"Things? What sort of things, but?"

"Just small parcels."

"Bombs?"

The old man yawned, his jaws falling open like a shark's.

Rocky considered the matter. "What yer want *me* to do it for, but? Yer could get anybody. . ."

"You're inconspicuous."

Insulted, Rocky lost his fear and pushed his hand through his red hair angrily. "Yer can take dat back, mister! *And* yer bargain! Get de scuffers on de phone! I'll go ter jail!"

The man gave that squawking laugh again. "Inconspicuous because you're obvious – everybody round here knows you, don't they?"

Rocky couldn't deny it. "Well," he said with a certain amount of satisfaction, "I'm the leader of the Cats' Gang, an' I've done Chick's Lot twice, an'—"

"Payment for each trip."

"Wur's de trips to, but?"

"In the neighbourhood."

"What's it worth?"

"Five pounds a trip."

Rocky couldn't believe it. He could make a fortune

without having to get the loot out of the house and then having to get the Nabber to unload it. There had to be a catch.

"If yer not inter explosives, why can't yer do it yerself? Yer wander round enough."

"My business. Come back a week today. Same time. Front door. Special ring," and he started chanting and waving a long forefinger: "One-two-three-four-five, Can you catch a fish alive?"

Rocky glowered at him. "You tryin' ter take the mickey?" he demanded.

"Five. Five rings. At the door. . ."

He was free and running towards home through the dark, empty streets, and then climbing through the window into his bedroom. But he wasn't free, he thought, as he lay in bed. Might never be. That old man had outwitted him at every turn, and he didn't even know what he was into now. The other problem was what to tell the Cats.

"I gorrin," he told them, sounding triumphant. "Told youse I would. An' der place – it *stinks*! An' it's full of rats an' rubbish – an' cold – yer wuddent believe it!"

"We don't," said the Nabber.

"Listen – this is the truth. I gorrin—"

"What yer got out den? Out of de place?"

Rocky did a quick think. "Didn't get nothin' dis time, but next time, I'll suss der place. Said I wouldn't tell anybody, but he's give me a job de

Ratman, deliverin' things. Five pounds a time!"

"An I believe in Daddy Christmas," said the Nabber.

"I'll do yer, Nabber! It's the truth! I'm tellin' yer!"

"What sort of things does he want you to deliver?" asked Billy.

"He didn't say."

"Could be very heavy things," said Chan. "How would you carry them?"

"Wouldn't do it, Rocky," advised Billy. "Yer have ter know what yer deliverin'."

"S'not explosives, but!"

"Stolen goods?" suggested Beady.

"What'd he want to have stolen goods for? He's got enough stuff in der. And listen, I'll do it for a bit, just so I can keep on sussin' the place an' find out how we can get in – could maybe open a window."

"What's he want yer ter do deliveries for?" put in the Nabber. "That's what puzzles me."

"Says I'm inconspicuous."

"What? You? Yer as inconspicuous as a jam-butty car with its sirens goin'!"

"Yer thick as two planks, Nabber Neville! I'm inconspicuous because everybody knows me, see? Dey expect ter see me round. Like . . . like . . ."

"Like the postman, or the milk feller," suggested Billy helpfully.

"Yer've got it, wack!"

"Funny, that," said the Nabber reflectively, "because I've never seen McMahon questioning a milk feller

117

and takin' him in. And anyway, howd' yer get into the house?"

"Told yer. The doors wasn't locked."

"And the old feller was inside?"

"No – he come in afterwards—"

"And nabbed yer – set a trap, didn't he? Got yer fixed. Blackmailing yer, in't he?"

"What yer mean?"

"Obvious, in't it?"

And it was obvious to all of them.

The Cats eventually drifted away, not happy about the situation, but the Nabber stayed on for a bit with Rocky, watching the clouds being driven over the Cathedral as the wind got up and turned cold, both of them thinking the same thing.

At last the Nabber said, "Yer have to admit it – he's got yer hooked, hasn't he? An' yer a courier an' don't know what yer carryin'."

"I'll fix him, but," said Rocky ferociously.

"Tell yer what," offered the Nabber generously, but mainly because he was curious, "when yer go next time, I'll come wid yer. Could always keep a look-out."

Rocky was grateful. "Great," he said. "Let yer know the date an' time." But he already knew the date and time – the Ratman was very precise.

"That's unless I've got somethin' on," said the Nabber, covering himself.

"Knew I could rely on yer," said Rocky sarcastically. "See yer den!"

"See yer!"

But as he went into Number 3, Rocky was thinking that the Nabber couldn't be much help anyway – the old man *had* got him.

For once, Mrs Flanagan and Suzie weren't fighting each other. It was all peace and tranquillity in the flickering light from the television, the red glow from the electric fire and the light from the ceiling lamp – it gave a sense of safety. Suzie was squatting, mesmerised, in front of the television set, and Mrs Flanagan was relaxed in her chair with her feet on the stool. "That you, luv?" she asked. "Yer late. Wur've yer been?"

"Just around." Rocky dropped on to the sofa and fixed his eyes on the television screen, but not seeing it, just going over the situation he was in. Sort of a slave for ever to that old man. And there had to be something criminal about this business of delivering things. Must be loot – maybe antique loot. Couldn't be a bag of groceries.

And if the scuffers got on to it, *he'd* be the one they'd come after. It was all right, he concluded, arranging a job yourself, but it was no good having it arranged for you, and having to carry the can back.

"What's der ter eat?" he asked irritably.

"Could make yerself a dog butty, and der's some pickles and crisps," said Mrs Flanagan.

Rocky was amazed, and his spirits climbed several rungs. "Great! Haven't had corned beef since Flanagan was here!" And he went to collect the necessary ingredients. "Had yours, Suzie?" he asked in passing.

Suzie nodded.

"What yer watchin'?"

Suzie looked at him with dazed eyes. "That," she said, pointing to the television set. It was some soap opera that was engrossing his mother, but Rocky didn't think Suzie was taking in a thing.

As he ate the dog butty, he became convinced that things weren't as bad as he'd thought. The old man couldn't keep a grip on him for long, he'd make a bit of money out of it, and he'd be able to suss the house out properly and get some things out of it. He wouldn't let the old man defeat him. Would be all right, he decided, and then realised that his mother was looking different.

"Yer've had yer hair done," he said suddenly and accusingly. "An' yer've gorra new dress."

"Wondered when yer'd notice." Mrs Flanagan sat up, patting her hair. "What yer think?"

"What's it for, but? S'not Christmas yet."

"Flanagan's comin' back. He really is."

"Well, I'll need a new anorak and some jeans. Dese have got holes in dem, an' Flanagan wouldn't like it, would he? An' Suzie could do with—"

"Didn't say I'd won the Pools!" Mrs Flanagan was indignant. "Just said Flanagan was comin'!"

"When?"

"Here." Mrs Flanagan took a postcard from behind the alarm clock on the mantelpiece and handed it to Rocky. It was a picture of some Chinese in front of a Chinese restaurant. On the back Flanagan had written. "On my way. Back soon."

"On his way, see," said Mrs Flanagan complacently. "So I'm startin' ter get the place cleaned up termorrer, and yer'll have ter help."

"He said the same last time, an' he didn't come, but." Rocky studied the small print on the card. It said 'Happy World Restaurant, Bukit Timah Road, Singapore'.

"He's goin' the wrong way," he said.

"What yer on about?"

"Flanagan. He's goin' the wrong way. The last card was from the Mediterranean, but dis one's from Singapore. That's further away – in the wrong direction."

Mrs Flanagan snatched the card from him. "That's a lot of rubbish! He says he's comin' home."

"Said it before, didn't he? But he's goin' in der wrong direction. Maybe he's doin' a round-the-world. Comin' back through Australia."

"On a tanker?" demanded Mrs Flanagan.

Rocky shrugged. "Looks like it."

Mrs Flanagan glared at Rocky, then stalked away to get her coat out of the cupboard, kicked off her slippers and put on some high-heeled shoes.

"I'm goin' out," she said.

"Dis time of night?" asked Rocky.

"Goin' ter yer Auntie Chrissie's. You put *her* ter bed and get ter bed yerself – and mind yer put the telly off."

"But, mam. . ."

The door slammed behind her, and after a few moments Suzie said with some satisfaction, "Gone, Rocky."

"Yes, tatty-'ead," said Rocky. "She's gone." And as he studied the postcard from Flanagan, he wished his stepfather *was* back so that he could talk to him about the Ratman. Then he thought, forget it – he's not coming back. Ever. Can do without him, anyway. And I'll beat the nutter, he thought. At his own game. I'll beat our Joey as well.

He was being chased by a black coffin with the Ratman's head on top and his arms sticking out of the sides, stretching towards him. He was thinking that it was very strange that a coffin could get along as fast as that by itself, and he knew it was catching up on him, because there was something wrong with his legs. They were moving, but not getting him anywhere. Then he felt a hand on his shoulder, and shouted "Geroff!" and sat up in bed.

Suzie was sitting up in the other bed, saying, "Rocky! Rocky!" He shook his head to get rid of the nightmare.

Suzie asked anxiously, "Hurt, Rocky?"

"Not hurt, yer rubbish. Here, what's der time? Wur's me mam?" He had a feeling that it was later than they usually got up.

"Get yer things on, tatty-'ead," he ordered, and went into the next room. He unpinned the curtains and pulled them back. His mam wasn't there. Looked as if she hadn't been there all night, and the clock on

122

the mantelpiece seemed to have reached the decision that the time was half past eight – though that decision could date back to last night.

He ran back to his bedroom and started throwing on clothes. "We're late, Suzie. Come on!"

As they went into the passageway, Ellen-from-upstairs peered down at them. "Something wrong, Rocky?" she asked urgently. "Suzie been hurt?"

"She's all right. . ."

"But somebody was shouting."

"We're late but, Ellen!"

In Larkspur Lane, he shot into the newsagent's and seized two Yorkie bars. "Have dese, missus," he said.

"An' de money?" the woman behind the counter snarled at him.

"That's it – go on, put it in yer savings bank!"

The Cats were not in sight, which confirmed the fact that they were late.

"Here's yer breakfast, tatty-'ead," he shouted to Suzie, handing her a Yorkie bar.

"No – Fizzy Cakes an' Crocodiles!" Suzie protested from two yards behind him, the bow of ribbon in her hair preparing to take off and her face twisted in protest.

"Yer can't have *dem* for breakfast. Yer can only have dem for yer dinner!"

He pushed a protesting and indignant Suzie into her part of the school and eventually, amid cheers, got into his own classroom.

His form master that year was a man called Mr Darrell, who had a hard line in sarcasm. Rocky and he had been sworn enemies from their first meeting.

"You're late, Rocky O'Rourke," he said. It wasn't an accusation, it was a statement of fact.

"Not late, sir," said Rocky innocently. "I'm early for der matinee, see," which received due acknowledgement from the class. And *darrell* do you, Darrell, Rocky thought.

He then received an invitation from Mr Darrell to visit him in the classroom at morning break. But even that prospect couldn't keep his mind on maths, in which Mr Darrell excelled. He was worried about the fix he was in with the Ratman, and about his mother's disappearance. If she didn't come back, they could *both* be put in a home – him *and* Suzie. Probably different homes.

"What are you *doing*?" Mr Darrell's voice broke into his thoughts.

"Nothin', sir. Wasn't doin' nothin'!"

"You're not here to do nothing."

"Well, I don't know," said Rocky. "I'm wrong when I'm doin' somethin', and I'm wrong when I'm doin' nothin'! Could yer make the rules clearer like?"

His interview with Mr Darrell was not a pleasant one and, feeling fed up and worried, he left the school at lunchtime without speaking to the Cats, collected an astonished but willing Suzie and went home.

Trevor was sitting in his pram outside Number 3, looking a bit subdued, but when Rocky gave his pram a friendly rock he gave Rocky a friendly shake of his tin

124

with the dried peas in it, and they went into Number 3. To Rocky's relief, his mother was sitting in her chair, looking a bit pale, and Ellen-from-upstairs was pouring her a cup of tea.

"What you two doin' here?" demanded Mrs Flanagan, shocked.

"Come ter see where yer were."

"Yer should be in the school."

"Come ter see where yer were," repeated Rocky, and dropped down on to the sofa.

"He's bound to've been worried, Mrs Flanagan," said Ellen. "S'only natural."

"Yer'll not have had yer dinners, but," objected Mrs Flanagan. "An' I'm in no state ter get them."

"I'll find somethin', Mrs Flanagan, and yer can let me have it back."

"S'all right, Ellen, luv. He can go down ter Chan's. Yer know, Ellen, it's just Flanagan not comin' back."

"Mrs Flanagan, I've been deserted once," and Ellen sniffed, "an' I'm likely ter be deserted again – an' I've always done me best – so I know how yer feel."

"Well, we'll stick together, Ellen," concluded Mrs Flanagan, "an' yer'll have yer dinner wid us. Rocky'll go down ter Chan's – my treat." That cheered them all up considerably.

"An' bring Trevor in here an', Rocky, put der plates in the oven before yer go." Then she added, to herself, "Oh, my head."

It was a change having Ellen and Trevor for dinner, and fish and chips, and his mam *had* been generous.

125

In fact Suzie fell asleep on the sofa afterwards, and Mrs Flanagan started dozing in her chair until Rocky, moving restlessly round the room, wakened her.

"What yer doin'?" she asked.

"Not doin' nothin'."

"Well, sit down."

"Can't just keep sittin' down."

"Well, go out. . ."

"Where to, but?"

Mrs Flanagan had a sudden inspiration. "Here," she said. "Der's presents for youse two from yer Auntie Chrissie. Forgot about dem. In that carrier, over there."

Rocky found the carrier and looked inside.

"Dey're just wellies," he objected.

"Dey're not, see. Dey're special. Dey're mukluks. Yer can use dem anywhere – on de moon, even."

Rocky pulled his pair on – they were bright blue, and had thick soles. Suzie woke up and put her pair on – they were bright red, and had thick soles.

"Hi, Suzie," said Rocky. "Dese are moon-boots – come on!"

He started prancing round the room, with Suzie following, making high steps until his mother shouted, "Will yer stop it! Yer makin' me head thump!"

"Here, was nice of me Auntie Chrissie," said Rocky.

"Don't know about that. She got them cheap from a feller that come round the doors."

"Wur's she live, me Auntie Chrissie?"

126

"Never mind about that. An' yer can both get yerselves outside in them mukluks, and let me have some peace!"

They went down to Larkspur Lane, because there was just a chance that the Cats might have arrived on their way home from school, and Rocky wanted to show off his mukluks. The Cats *were* there, hanging round Pa Richardson's.

The Nabber took one look at Rocky and Suzie, and shuddered and covered his eyes with his hands. "Don't believe it," he groaned. "The wellies – can't bear ter look at them!"

"Not wellies, big mouth. Mukluks. From me Auntie Chrissie, see?"

"Yer mean yer've got relatives? Thought your family was confined to the lot at Number 3. It's worryin', that is, the idea of more of yer."

"Dey're all right, the mukluks," said Beady. "All yer need now is some wet weather ter try them out in."

"Could try them out in the bath," suggested Little Chan.

"Don't have baths at Number 3," said the Nabber.

"Listen, Nabber," said Rocky, "you save yer breath for tomorrer night – I'm goin' inter the Ratman's."

The Nabber became reflective. "Well, I'm not sure. . ."

"Scared?"

"I'll show yer!"

"Right, den!"

127

"Darrell's after yer, Rocky," said Billy, "for saggin' this afternoon."

"Wur'd yer go to anyway?" asked the Nabber.

"My business. . . Hi, look at the man!"

Pa Richardson's nephew was glaring at them from inside the shop, and as they started laughing he came out, indignant.

"Clear off, you lot!" he ordered. "Public nuisances, you are!"

"Seen any more cowboys?" asked Rocky.

"I've told yer to—"

"Hi, when's he comin' back, yer uncle?"

"Soon as I can drag him here."

"Not makin' this place into a little Spar shop, den?"

"With you lot around?"

He went back into the shop, slamming the door.

"Gets himself into a state, doesn't he?" said Rocky. "It's worth standing round here just ter see him."

CHAPTER

8

"I'll wait here an' keep dowse," said the Nabber, stopping on the opposite side of Crown Street to the Ratman's house, and close to the alley that led back to St Catherine's Square.

"See yer not takin' any risks!" said Rocky contemptuously.

"I am, but. Murky Evans is back. He could come along here."

"What'll yer do if he does?"

The Nabber considered. "Well, if I shout ter warn you, it would warn him as well."

"Yer could hoot like a owl, like Billy does."

But the Nabber obviously considered that this was beneath the dignity of him and his hat, which he was wearing again.

"Ferget it!" said Rocky, disgusted.

"No, listen. If der's any danger, I'll cross over an' ring the bell."

Rocky shrugged. Didn't matter much. He was the one facing the Ratman. He went across to the house, paused to get his courage up, then gave the secret ring at the door. Nothing happened.

"Is he out?" The Nabber's voice came cautiously across the street.

But he wasn't. Something moved behind one of the windows at the side of the door, then a key turned in a lock, a chain dropped and the door opened, slowly and slightly, and Rocky saw the long, narrow face of the Ratman, white, with bright eyes.

"Enter," he said.

Rocky squeezed through the narrow opening, and was engulfed again in the darkness, the smell, the scratchings and patterings.

"Wur yer, mister?" he asked.

The Ratman switched on a dim light and led the way along the passage to the room where the easy chair was. The curtains were drawn, and only the small table lamp on the desk gave any light. It was cold, very cold, but in his overcoat and scarf the Ratman didn't seem to feel it. He unfolded himself like a deck chair and sat down.

"There's inns and ins," he started. "And dye and die, and. . ."

"Listen, mister," said Rocky desperately, "me feet's freezin' ter the floor. Will yer belt up, an' let's have what yer want delivered."

The Ratman's mouth split into a wide grin, as he enjoyed Rocky's anxiety. Then he lifted something from beside his chair, and shouting, "Catch!" threw a football at Rocky.

Rocky caught it, looked at it and protested, "Coddin' me, aren't yer? Big joke, in't it?"

"No joke. You deliver it. Joseph Terrace. The

130

Buildings. Number 23." He leaned forward, still smiling, tapped his nose with a long forefinger and winked.

"Listen, mister," said Rocky. "S'not on. That's Chick's territory. I'm not goin' inter it for five quid ter deliver a football. Think I've gorra holler head?"

"That was the deal – deliver, and no court. Or caught, and court."

Rocky thought about it. Main thing was to get out of that house. "Right. Give us de money. An' I'm not doin' dis again!"

"It was a deal. Next week, same time, special ring." The Ratman stood up, towering over Rocky, and went to the desk. Rocky, looking at the cobwebs on the ceiling, felt like a trapped fly. Then he saw that the nutter had unlocked a drawer in the desk, and that the drawer was packed tight with money. The Ratman saw that Rocky had seen the money, and a funny look came on his face, like Punch when he was going to beat up Judy.

"Wait in the passage," said the Ratman.

Rocky went out hastily towards the front door. As he waited, wondering how he could get out of the nutter's grip, another idea came to him. He was alone and there was the window at the side of the door, one that would slide up and had a catch halfway up, like the ones at home: and there was that drawer full of money.

A pickpocket at Aintree racecourse when everybody was watching the Grand National couldn't have moved quicker. One hand stretched up and released the catch, and Rocky was standing at the other side of the door when the Ratman came down the passage to him.

"One football, five pounds, and three makes Number twenty-three, and seven days makes next week," he chanted.

Rocky shoved the note into his pocket and took a last look at that face – because he didn't intend seeing it again.

"Unlock der door, will yer? I've got a important appointment," he said.

"So you have," said the Ratman. "So you have."

The Nabber was strategically placed just on the corner that led to St Catherine's Square and safety, and Rocky didn't see him as he ran past, but the Nabber came after him, shouting, "What happened?"

"Not hangin' about!"

They stopped in St Catherine's Square, breathing hard.

"What yer get, den?" the Nabber panted. "What did he give yer?"

"This." Rocky held out the five-pound note.

"Wur's the parcel, but?"

"No parcel – was this," and Rocky held out the football.

He knew what would happen. The Nabber, after a minute, was bent double with laughter, slapping his hat against his leg, cowboy fashion, and making appropriate cowboy noises. Rocky sat down on the wall and watched him.

Ellen-from-upstairs's window slid open and she looked out. "Who's there?" she asked anxiously.

"Just me an' the Nabber, Ellen," said Rocky.

"All right, are youse?"

"All right, an' thanks very much for askin'."

The Nabber then subsided. "Well," he concluded, "s'been an' interestin' evening. I'll get off. Yer've done all right, with the five pounds and the football. Wur d'yer have ter deliver it?" He fell about again.

"Joseph's."

That sobered the Nabber considerably. "Yer can't risk goin' round there ter deliver a football for five pounds. They'll have yer – think *you* was a nutter. Forget it. Throw it away an' tell him yer delivered it. He'll never know. Here, let's have it, an' I'll send it down as far as Paddy's Wigwam. . . or we could kick it inter Joseph Buildings an' that'll be that. Another waste of time, like everything yer get into. Settin' us up to get inter empty shops, and gettin' loot out of the Rialto and havin' ter take it back again, an'—"

"Shurrup, ear-basher, an' give yer brains a rest. He's a nutter all right, but he's not mental. Der'll be somethin' inside this."

"Yer mean like der Crown Jewels?" asked the Nabber sarcastically.

"Could be silver an' gold things – he's got enough of dem." Rocky tossed the ball up and down experimentally. It didn't help.

"What'd he send silver an' gold things ter Joseph's for, but?"

"A fence?"

133

"Listen," said the Nabber, in the manner of one who knows what he's talking about, "the only things yer can unload in Joseph's is ciggies an' shirts an' tins of meat an' trannies an'. . ."

"All right well. So *you* can't unload gold an' silver?"

The Nabber reflected. "Me dad might," he said. "But he's not back yet."

"He's got a drawer full of money, the nutter," said Rocky. "Saw it. Stacked wid it."

That encouraged the Nabber. "Real, is it? Not Monopoly?"

"I fixed a window ter get in through, and he doesn't know."

That stunned the Nabber for a bit, then he said, "When'll we do it?"

"Have ter be when he's out at night."

They both thought about it. The Nabber thought about whether he should risk it, and Rocky thought about the Ratman and what he could be up to. Then he said, "Nabber, what about 'smack'?"

"Yer not inter that?"

"*He* could be. . ."

"The Ratman?"

"Could be." Rocky stood up and kicked the ball against the wall of Number 3, just as Ellen-from-upstair's husband was passing and had to do a sidestep to avoid it.

"Would you like to kick that ball around in some other place?" he asked, furious.

"Wur d'yer suggest?" asked the Nabber, wanting information.

"The Sahara!" And he went into Number 3.

"S'dried up – like you!" Rocky shouted after him, and felt better about things, but then he began to worry about the football, turning it round in his hands, trying to see if there was any place that looked as though it might have been opened, and something put in.

The Nabber stood up. "Well," he said. "I'll geroff an' leave yer wid yer problem."

"That's brill, in't it? Brill! Everything's all right as long as *I'm* taking the risks and you're—"

"Now then, wacks, bit late for footy, in't it?" a voice said, and they were both anxious. It wasn't McMahon, however, but the wingy, a bit merry from the pub. "That a new ball, Rocky? Yer mam got it for yer?"

"No, Mr Oliver," Rocky said quickly. "S'the Nabber's," and he threw the ball at the Nabber, who caught it, considered things for a moment and then said,

"Yer can borrow it for a bit," and threw it back as if it was burning his fingers. "Terrah well. See youse," he said, and went off into the darkness at a fast pace.

The wingy sat down beside Rocky. "Nabber's not generally as generous," he said.

"Depends," said Rocky, "on the circumstances." Could be disaster for him, that football, he thought, wondering whether he should confide in the wingy and ask his advice. But that would mean confessing that he'd gone into the Ratman's house, and the wingy would go spare over that. But there was nobody else to talk to about it.

"Listen, Mr Oliver," he said.

"What is it, Rocky?"

"Nothin', yer know like."

"Well, if yer've nothin' to say, I'll clear off." Mr Oliver stood up and then said, "Yer not in trouble, Rocky? Yer'd tell me, wuddent yer, if yer was?"

"Course I would, Mr Oliver."

"Right. I'm off."

Which left Rocky alone with the problem.

He was just about to go into Number 3 when a motor bike roared into the Square, its headlight blinding. It stopped outside Number 3, and the leather-jacketed driver in his white helmet revved up ear-shatteringly a few times, which brought the woman from Number 4 out, yelling, "Clear off, or I'll have the police ter you!"

Ellen-from-upstairs's window was pushed up, and her husband put his head out and shouted, "Stop that noise!"

Joey revved up again, and another bike with a headlight arrived, in charge of a figure sparkling with silver badges, who also did some revving up.

"Hi, Joey!" shouted Rocky, forgetting his troubles in the general pandemonium.

"Hi, der, our kid!"

"What's goin' on? What's all der noise?" Mrs Flanagan, in slippers, asked from the doorstep of Number 3.

"Hi, mam! S'me!" and Joey switched off his engine.

"Yer back, Joey luv! An' is dis yer friend?" she asked, trying to see the friend through his headlight. He seemed a dramatic figure but, whoever he was, he didn't stay. He turned his bike and roared off, and the Square became relatively peaceful except for an argument between Mrs Flanagan and the woman from Number 4 and Ellen-from-upstairs's husband, who were all indignant and angry.

"Yer can shurrup!" Mrs Flanagan told the woman from Number 4. "I can have *you* put away any time. An' *you*," she shouted up at Ellen-from-upstairs's husband, "I'm watchin' *you*! *An'* yer carryin' on, an' I'll have the social worker round if that baby keeps on cryin'."

This seemed to settle both of them, and Mrs Flanagan swept triumphantly into Number 3. Rocky followed with the football which, he thought, could be a kind of time-bomb.

"I'm not stayin', mam," Joey was saying as they went in.

"Why not, but?" Mrs Flanagan was dismayed. "Yer *never* stayin'!"

"Can't help it. It's the job. I'm stayin' wid me mate – the feller on the bike. We're organisin' it."

Mrs Flanagan sank into her chair. "I don't know," she said. "What wid you and Flanagan – always off after yer jobs. . ."

"What about Flanagan?" Joey was anxious.

"Not back yet. Don't know when he'll be."

"Who's yer mate, and what's de job?" asked Rocky.

"Yer'll get ter know yet. Anyways, I'm off. See yer again, mam." And Joey was gone.

"He's a good lad," concluded Mrs Flanagan. "He does his best. Yer know, Rocky, I think our

137

Joey could make it yet. He seems ter be on ter somethin'."

Rocky sat down on the sofa. "Inter somethin', yer mean," he muttered.

"What's that, luv?" his mother asked, switching on the telly.

Suzie appeared from behind the sofa. "Rocky," she whispered, "pies," and held out two small ones.

"Wur'd'yer get *them* from?" Rocky asked.

Suzie smiled, and said, "Take."

"Now, listen, Suzie, yer'll have ter stop that. S'all right for me, see, ter do that, but *you* haven't got to. Got it?"

"Got it," and Suzie bit into her pie.

"Pa Richardson's, in't it," asked Rocky, chewing. "Always four weeks old."

He looked at the football that lay beside him on the sofa. Had to be excavated, he decided. Had to be.

Little Chan was very seriously handing out mugs of tea to the members of the Cats Gang, who were sitting round the card table in the hideout. Each of them helped himself in turn to a spoonful of conny out of the tin and a biscuit from a packet Beady had again found lying on the pavement. They didn't look at the tea or the conny or the biscuits. They were looking at the football Rocky had cut open and disembowelled. It had contained some paper for packing, and a plastic bag filled with a greyish-white powder.

"That's it," said Beady at last. "I'm clearin' off. If that's smack, and the scuffers raid this place, me

138

mam'll batter me ter Birkenhead an' back an' put me remains in the dustin! So terrah. . ."

"Scuffers don't know de stuff is here, but," said the Nabber.

"Nobody knows it's here," said Rocky.

"The Ratman knows he give it to yer," said Beady.

"He's not goin' ter tell the scuffers about it, but."

"The pusher in Joseph's, Rocky," said Billy. "He's goin' ter make inquiries when it doesn't arrive."

"I'll see ter him. Want ter know who he is, anyway," said Rocky.

Billy frowned down at his mug of tea. "What if de scuffers suspect the Ratman? They could have been watchin' him – McMahon saw us that night. . ."

"Was just chance," said Rocky. "Just happened ter be prowlin' round ter fill in der time – that's what dey do, scuffers. Dey don't suspect the Ratman – they're all sorry for him. Wouldn't believe he'd be in to anything like this. Can't believe it meself, because he seems ter have a bit of a vacancy above his neck."

"Well," said the Nabber, leaning back and looking clever, "done all right, in't yer? *He* gives yer five quid ter deliver it, an' *you* lift it. Worth a fortune, that lot. How'll yer market it? Got a plan? 'Cos yer generally have a plan, don't yer? One of dem that always goes wrong."

"We're not playin' space games, Nabber," said Rocky.

"No. We're not," said Beady.

139

"Yer not goin' ter sell it, Rocky?" said Billy.

"He's got to! Worth a fortune! Thousand quid at least!" the Nabber exclaimed.

"Could be twenty years' sentence, if they find this stuff here," said Little Chan solemnly. "You would be over thirty when you got out. Unless there was remission."

They contemplated this statement in silence.

Then Billy asked, "What *will* yer do, Rocky?"

Rocky sat back, pushed his hand through his red hair and said, "Don't worry, skin. Know what I'll do. It'll go back to the Ratman."

The Nabber groaned. "Oh no! Yer not! Yer not listenin' to gammy leg here!"

"You mind yer lip, Nabber, when yer talkin' about Billy. He's a good skin – better than you are. Yer can *depend* on Billy."

"Yer wantin' some experience?" And the Nabber stood up and put his fists up. "Come on – I'll give yer some!"

"Take six men an' a special blessin'," said Rocky, contemptuously. "An' sit down an' give yer chin a rest. I've *got* the Ratman, see? He's played inter me hands. He give me the smack ter deliver an' he told me where to deliver it, so I'm checkin' on that place an' then, when the Ratman's out, I'm puttin' the smack back in his house, an' if he ever comes back at me, I'll tell him ter lay off or I'll scat on him *and* his pusher ter the scuffers!"

Rocky was triumphant: then amazed at the lack of response.

"What's up wid youse?" he demanded. "Tellin' youse – it's all worked out. An' there's a drawer full of money to be emptied – enough ter buy that revolving restaurant on the Post Office tower!"

"Not revolvin' now but," said Beady pessimistically.

Rocky ignored this. "Need some gloves, Nabber," he said, "when we take der smack back. Don't want ter leave fingerprints."

"*You* don't."

"You don't, neither. Yer comin' as well. See yer," and he left the hideout, leaving them all apprehensive – especially the Nabber.

CHAPTER
9

At the beginning of Joseph Terrace, Rocky stopped and looked down the street for signs of trouble. At night time the Terrace was dangerous, but also mysterious, with the empty houses dark down one side and the lights and shouts from Joseph Buildings on the other, the pub and the off-licence attracting gangs like moths to a flame, and waste land beyond the empty houses black and dangerous. In daylight, however, the Terrace was generally back to normal, with the wind swirling dust and litter round any convenient corner, dandelions and other more exotic weeds and even grass sprouting between the uneven paving-stones which lay in wait to trip up the unsteady drunk or the unwary toddler, and generally a girl gazing blankly out through the window of the launderette as though she were a prisoner for life.

The Terrace did have its artistic side, though – the decorations and messages on the walls of the empty houses, which recorded many years of the history of the Terrace. 'Toothy Bedford was here', one message recorded, but 'Toothy Bedford was extracted', another recorded. There was a quite elaborate drawing of a man on a horse, beside which was written, 'King Billy is a hero – Boyne 1960', and then in large white-painted capitals, 'TO HELL WITH THE PRODDY DOGS', and then in large orange-painted capitals, 'DOWN WITH THE POPE'. Under a large notice saying 'DO NOT WRITE ON THIS WALL' in smaller letters and purple paint was a message for Arlene McLintock, promising that Dave Jameson would be waiting for her, same place, same time next year.

But there was still a hostile feeling coming from the loiterers on the corners, and a lot of noise and violence in the activities of some tiddlers who had captured an abandoned car and, having smashed all its windows, were walking and jumping on it and beating it with bricks and hammers and metal bars to the accompaniment of shrieks and shouts.

Surveying it, Rocky wished he'd asked Billy to come and keep dowse for him. He knew Billy would have, but he might have got hurt. He wished he hadn't come at all.

He started walking towards the staircase of the flats, knowing he was being watched and assessed, aware that the tiddlers weren't making quite so much noise, and that they were monitoring his progress. Just before he got to Number 23, on the third landing, a tiddler dashed past him and banged on one of the windows of Number 23. Nobody looked out, and the tiddler didn't stop.

Rocky rang the bell at Number 23, and as he waited the cave-insect boy came anxiously up to him.

"You deliverin'?" he whispered.

"What yer on about?" asked Rocky.

143

"Give us some smack an' I'll sell yer some gear. Real cheap. Got all kinds. Could get yer anythin'."

"Haven't got any smack," said Rocky, which was true. "Clear off."

"But I'll bring der loot to yer, if yer'll give me some. . ."

The door of the flat opened, and a plump, bright woman, wearing a plastic apron with 'Mum's the word' on it, smiled at them.

"Hello, Mickey. Come for Dan? An' are you a new friend?" she asked Rocky. "I can't keep up wid his friends, he's got that many, Dan has. Hi, Dan!" she shouted into the flat, "yer friends is here."

After a few moments a tall, slim boy of about sixteen, very smart in a navy blazer and trousers and white shirt, came casually out to them. He had a lot of black hair cut in neat style, and he was smiling. But Rocky immediately distrusted him, because his eyes were pale and expressionless and he said, "Clear off," not looking at Mickey, but meaning him.

Mickey began a kind of whine – "Dan, but Dan, he's—"

"Off!"

Mickey retreated a few yards and Dan said, "Told yer ter keep off the Ratman."

"Was you, was it? Well, yer should of give that message ter the Ratman, shouldn't yer? Ter keep off *me*."

Dan assessed the situation. "All right. He got yer. Yer deliverin'?"

"That's right," said Rocky.

"Come in, then."

Rocky hesitated for a moment, but after all, he thought, Dan's mother was there. Nothing could happen. He couldn't be attacked or anything. So he followed Dan into a room off the passage. Rocky was staggered. "S'Buckingham Palace," he muttered. It was luxurious: fitted carpet, green velvet curtains, a divan with black and white striped pillows and duvet-cover, a polished desk with a typewriter, two white easy chairs and a radio centre. A bit different from Rocky's bedroom in Number 3.

Dan sat down behind the desk and indicated a chair to Rocky.

"I cuddent," said Rocky, "cuddent sit on that. Might mess it up! Stay on me feet." Which he thought was safer, anyway. "Doin' well, aren't yer?"

"Let's have the—" But the door opened, and his mother smiled at them.

"Nice, isn't it," she said to Rocky. "Paid for it all out of his pocket money and doing odd jobs."

"Mam, will yer clear off?" demanded Dan.

"Just thought yer might like some coffee. . . Well, if yer change yer minds. . ." and she departed.

"The smack," said Dan, unemotionally but threateningly.

"Smack? Haven't got none."

"From the Ratman. . ."

"Didn't give me none." Rocky was all innocence.

Dan's face hardened. "Nobody fools around with me. Yer here deliverin' for the Ratman, or you wouldn't be here. And if yer thinkin' of pushing it yerself – forget it. Nobody'll buy, and I've got a

145

lot of friends who'll see that you come out of hospital permanently disabled. Now, hand it over."

"Well," said Rocky, "only thing he give me was this." He held out the football. "Thought it must be a present to yer."

"He gets the weirdest ideas. Hand it over and sit down while I make sure yer haven't done a switch." He must have noticed some reaction of Rocky's that increased his suspicions, because he said, "Yer have, haven't yer? Done a switch? Well, yer'll not get out of here—"

Just then, there was a scratching on the window, and he turned to look. Mickey could just be seen mistily, anxious and pleading, through the Terylene curtains.

"Here!" said Rocky. "Catch!" He threw the football, and as Dan twisted round to catch it, Rocky dashed for the door, into the passage and out, and started for the stairs. He heard Dan shout something, and a shrill whistle from Mickey, and when he got to the landing below he caught a quick glimpse of some of the loiterers on the corner moving fast towards the Buildings and of the tiddlers, mesmerised, around the car, from whose interior a thread of smoke was drifting. He took the next flight of stairs three at a time. But in the street he couldn't get through a crowd of people who were watching the tiddlers' progress with the car, so he dropped to the ground and wriggled round among their feet until he got to the front. Nobody noticed him – everybody was too interested in the black smoke and orange flames coming out of the car windows and every hole and crack in its bodywork. The tiddlers

146

were standing well back, awed by the results of their handiwork.

Then a voice shouted, "That's him – gerrim!" and Rocky saw three big fellows starting to push their way through to him. He didn't see how he could escape, but suddenly there was a roar of flame from the car, a noise as deafening as a low-flying jet, and most of the car went into the air and began returning to Joseph Terrace in pieces of various sizes, all hot.

As the crowd shouted and scattered in panic, Rocky took his chance and raced past the inferno, feeling the heat burn his skin, and ran on down the Terrace. At the corner he paused to look back. It was chaos, and nobody was following him, but as he started running again, a voice shouted, "Told you – trouble comin'."

It was Howard, still on his skates.

"Already come, Nelson!"

Ellen-from-upstairs was just getting Trevor out of his pram. "'Lo, der, Rocky," she said. "Yer look hot. Been runnin', have yer?"

Rocky stopped, panting, and stared at her, his red hair bristling and not quite sure yet that he'd got home safely.

"Me mam in?"

"She went out. Took a lot of things to the launderette. Been cleanin' all mornin'. Didn't see her, but I heard her. An' der's been a fire in Joseph's – look, yer can still see the smoke over St Catherine's. . ."

"She lock the door?" asked Rocky desperately.

"No. She come ter tell me she was takin' Suzie, and not lockin' the door, because yer'd be back soon, or your Joey would – can't remember now. Flanagan due back, is he?"

"Flanagan? We don't know."

"Well, he must be. What's she cleanin' for else?" Ellen went drearily into Number 3.

"All right, Ellen?" Rocky shouted up the stairs after her.

"Been better," was the reply.

He felt safe in the flat at first, until he noticed the cleanliness – lino, carpet, table, clock, cooker and sink – and the bed stripped. What was she up to now, his mam?

He looked out of the window, but there were no strangers in the Square, and from feeling hot, he suddenly felt cold, switched the fire on and sat in front of it, shivering. He knew he was in a right mess, but he hadn't really done anything wrong, except for going into the Ratman's. Now he would have Dan's heavies after him – wouldn't take Mickey long to find out where he lived, especially if he was promised some smack. And there was the heroin in the hideout.

Then he remembered something his father had said to him: "Brains is better than brawn. So if yer've got them – use them."

Well, he had. He'd got out of delivering the heroin, and he'd worked out how to take it back to the Ratman. But he'd have to lie very low until he could work out what to do about Dan.

"Back, are yer?" Mrs Flanagan came in, carrying a vast plastic bag full of washing, and followed by Suzie. She dropped the bag and sat down in her chair.

"There's a car on fire in Joseph Terrace. Seen it from the launderette. Two fire engines. Was stolen by some tiddlers. How d'they manage to drive them? I don't know. An' what's wrong wid you? Cat got yer tongue?"

"Haven't gorra cat, have we?"

"None of yer lip wid me!"

"Flanagan comin'? That why yer've been cleanin'?"

"No. S'not that. I made me mind up, see. I was in Ellen's this mornin', an' her place is like a picture, so I thought I've had enough of this – it'll be clean at least. But it'll all have ter be done up now – painted an' everythin'. But Flanagan'll have ter do that. I'm not getting up ladders. Yer Auntie Chrissie did that an' fell off, an' did herself a injury."

"What kind of a injury?" Rocky asked, interested in this added information about his Auntie Chrissie.

"That's none of your business. . ." Mrs Flanagan was beginning, when the door opened and Joey came in, all smiles and jubilation.

"Hello, mam! Hello, skin! How's things?"

"Joey, luv – come an' sit down! Didn't hear yer bike!"

"Haven't got it." Joey sat down, smirking.

"Yer've not smashed it up?" Mrs Flanagan was shocked.

"Sold it for scrap," suggested Rocky.

Joey winked at him. "Sold it. Not fer scrap. Ter buy a car, see."

"Yer gettin' a car? Oh, Joey!" Mrs Flanagan was delighted.

"That's right. Take youse out in it – ter the Wirral – one Sunday. An' here – this is for you, mam. Give yerself a treat wid it," and Joey, producing a wallet that seemed to be bursting with money, handed her three twenty-pound notes. Mrs Flanagan was impressed almost to the point of having the intuitions.

"Joey! Wur'd yer get it from?" she asked.

"I'm a rich man," said Joey modestly. "Here, our kid," and he handed Rocky three ten-pound notes.

Mrs Flanagan was overcome. "Yer have to give it to him," she sobbed, "if he's got the cash, he'll scatter it, not like some."

Rocky was puzzled. "Queen give yer a raise?" he asked.

"Can't help bein' a success."

"Which bank did you do?"

"That's enough of that," objected Mrs Flanagan. "It'll be from the job, in't it, Joey?"

"Dat's right. Things is goin' well."

"Job still goin', den?"

Joey looked a bit doubtful, then brightened up. "Stick wid me, wack, an' yer'll be in der gravy!" he advised.

"What about Suzie, den?" asked Rocky.

"What about her?"

"She's family – if it's a handout."

"She's not family," said Mrs Flanagan, "an' she doesn't need nothin'."

But Joey relented. "Yer can give her this," and he handed over two round pounds.

"Yer could make it five nicker."

"Why should he?" demanded Mrs Flanagan.

"'Cos he's rich," retorted Rocky, and because he *was* rich and didn't want it doubted, Joey handed over another three.

Apparently Joey couldn't stay, because he had business to attend to, so Mrs Flanagan went out with him to wave him off. Rocky sat down beside Suzie, who'd been quiet as a mouse with a cat in the neighbourhood while Joey had been there, drawing on a piece of paper with the red Biro.

"Here, Suzie," he said. "Present for yer from our Joey." He put the five pounds on the table.

Suzie obviously couldn't take this in.

"It's money, see? Put it in yer little red bag with the rest."

Suzie started to turn out the contents of the bag on to the table, but Rocky stopped her. "No, tatty-'ead. Yer don't want me mam ter see. Put it all in yer little bag, and when yer get the chance put it under the mattress on my bed – it'll be safe there. An' what yer drawin'?"

"House," said Suzie.

"Well, its walls is fallin' in an' it's gorra roof as crooked as a lush's hat."

Suzie scratched in a door. "Locked," she said. Then she drew in a window with a round, fierce face with black curly hair looking out. "*Her!*" she said. "Devil!"

Rocky hastily put his comic over the drawing as his mam came back, just in case she recognised the portrait. Mrs Flanagan drew the curtains and pinned them together with the safety pin, going on all the time about Joey and how clever he was, *and* generous, and how he would have a smashing business before long and get married to a nice girl. There was a pause while Mrs Flanagan thought up a mental picture of the nice girl and Joey's future home in Woolton, and put sausages on to fry and opened a tin of baked beans.

Rocky was only thinking that he'd better go down to Larkspur Lane and tell the Cats what had happened. It was the Steps that were worrying him, in case one of Dan's gang was waiting for him.

"Goin' out, Suzie," he said quietly.

"Come wid yer!" Suzie's face was desperate.

"No. Not be long. Just keep quiet, an' don't touch her books, an' get yer bag under my mattress." To his mother he said, "I'm off den, mam."

"Yer what? Wur to, but? Yer tea's ready!"

"S'business!"

"He's not comin'," said the Nabber, leaning against the windows of the newsagent's shop in Larkspur Lane. "The pusher's gang's got him. I told him. I told him ter just kick the football inter Joseph Terrace, but he wuddent listen. Never listens. Thinks he knows it all. . ."

He was irritating Beady, who wasn't often irritated. "Will yer stop janglin' on, Nabber?" he requested. "Could be dangerous for Rocky, this business."

152

"Well, I told him, but. . ."

"There was a fire in Joseph Terrace today," said Billy, frowning down at the handlebars of his bike.

"That's it! Dey burnt him!" said the Nabber.

"They could not do that," said Little Chan, shocked.

"Yer don't understand what he's into – yer don't—"

"'Lo, wacks!" Rocky joined them, a bit breathless after his race down the Steps, and relieved to be with them.

"What happened, Rocky?" asked Billy.

"Went all right. Found der feller – called Dan. Give him the empty football – he's makin' a fortune – should see his place. Then I had ter run – got his gang on ter me."

"They'll not forget yer," said the Nabber.

"Know that."

They all thought about this, and then Rocky said, "Anyway, next thing is ter take the smack back – an' I'll need youse all then. Tomorrer night. An' listen, our kid gave me this – thirty!"

"He give yer thirty?" The Nabber was incredulous.

"It is a lot of money," said Little Chan respectfully.

"Thought yer said he was mean, your Joey," said Beady.

"He is. But he's just showing off, see? Chuckin' it about, he is."

"Where did it come from?" asked Billy, frowning down at the handlebars of his bike and obviously worried about the whole thing.

Rocky shrugged. "He's not sayin'."

153

"Told yer," said the Nabber, "told yer yer should of got him ter cut us in. Told yer."

"An' I told you I knew he wouldn't. He's keepin' everythin' secret."

"Think he could have made all that honestly?" asked Billy.

"Honestly? Honestly?" The Nabber fell about laughing. "Yer jokin'! Honestly? Yer can't be that stupid!"

That hurt Billy, though he didn't say anything, but Rocky knew it and retorted, "Stupid? Billy, stupid? Yer one ter talk. Der was some nit nearly got nicked through pointing a imitation gun at—"

"All right. Belt up!" The Nabber hunched his shoulders in his camouflage jacket. "So what yer goin' ter do wid it all?"

"Could put a deposit on a BMX. Secondhand, like."

"An' how yer goin' ter pay the rest off?" asked the Nabber.

"What d'yer think *she* pays her paper boys?" asked Rocky, indicating the woman behind the counter in the newsagent's, who was watching them balefully.

"Not much," said Beady.

"Not enough to pay off a BMX," said Little Chan.

Rocky shrugged and glared in at the woman. "Yer probably right. Wouldn't give yer a spot if she had pimples. Here, I'm carryin' just now. Buy youse all chips an' Cokes."

They ate standing outside Chan's chippy, backs to the window, as it was warmer there than in the hideout at that time of night. They were discussing what Rocky

154

should do with the remainder of the thirty pounds – the Nabber suggesting that he should take a single ticket to Blackpool and jump off the pier, which Rocky said he would consider, since he was feeling quite happy and safe with the Cats round him – when a policeman came from the shadows and into the light from the chippy. It was Constable McMahon, who stopped in front of them, and had the benefit of seeing Little Chan's worried face peering over the counter, and Mrs Chan turning away from swirling chips in the pan of fat to watch what was happening. The half-dozen customers turned round as well.

Rocky took one look at him and felt less happy, though he didn't show it. He just ate another chip, and said, "'Lo der. Give yer the worst shift, did he, der sergeant?"

"Yer step-dad not back yet?"

"No. He's doin' a round-der-world in de wrong direction. Yer should try it." It was sheer nervousness that made Rocky cheeky. He was thinking of all the things McMahon could take him in for.

"I don't think Mrs Chan really wants an outdoor café here," said the constable, "so eat up and get home. Billy, is yer dad on night-shift?"

Billy nodded.

"Yer mam in?"

Billy nodded again.

"She'll be glad ter see yer back then. Yer'll leave the place tidy, won't yer? And who's payin' for the supper?"

"We're all muckin' in," said Rocky quickly.

155

"Right then. Yer'll all of gone home when I come back?"

As the constable went on along Larkspur Lane, the Cats had a definite sense of deflation, and the customers inside Chan's chippy turned round to watch the fish and chips being cooked, convinced that the action outside was over.

The Nabber screwed up his chip paper and dropped it, with an empty Coke can, into the litter basket. It wasn't like the Nabber to be so tidy.

"He's on ter yer," he said to Rocky.

"No, he's not. Just earnin' his keep bein' a scuffer. Easiest way ter earn a livin'. Hi," he added, having just had an idea, "think they'd take *me* on ter be a scuffer? What yer think? Make a good one, wuddent I?" He strutted round in front of the Cats. "Yer step–dad back yet?" he shouted at Billy, and "This is not a outdoor café and eat up an' get home an' wur's yer hat, Nabber?"

The Cats fell about.

"Could do it, cuddent I?" asked Rocky triumphantly.

"Well," said the Nabber, "yer not much good on the other side, so yer might as well try it. An' all the robbers in the neighbourhood'd have a field day!"

"Listen, Nabber," said Rocky ferociously, "yer can belt up, because yer comin' inter the Ratman's wid me tomorrow night, an' we'll see who's havin' a field day then!"

CHAPTER
10

"Stay here, an' I'll check the place," Rocky said quietly. He went to try the back door of the Ratman's house. It was locked, so he went round the corner to give the special ring at the bell. There was no answer, and nothing moved behind the window, so just to be sure everything would be all right, Rocky tried the window, in case it had been locked again. It hadn't. In fact, it was just the slightest bit open at the bottom. Rocky was suspicious. He was certain he hadn't opened it – just unlocked it. But maybe the Ratman had finally decided he could do with some fresh air.

The Cats waited anxiously in the alley. They were all very nervous. Billy's mouth was dry, and he kept on shivering; Little Chan just stood beside him, stiff with anxiety; Beady kept looking round nervously, listening for footsteps; and the Nabber hadn't a word to say for himself. What they were all thinking was what would happen if McMahon came by again. It wouldn't just be a warning this time. He would take them in, and then go into the house and maybe find the heroin. Their imaginations were working overtime on police stations, courtrooms, Black Marias, fines, jails, newspaper headlines, parents. . .

"If he's that clever, what's he need us around for," muttered the Nabber.

"We're the Cats," said Beady loyally. "Have ter stick tergether." Though he wished they hadn't got to.

"What's it always got ter be *his* glue for, but? An' he's all hot air, an' yer never know whether he knows what he's on about. . ."

Then Rocky returned, silent as a shadow. "S'all right," he said. "I give the special ring, and he didn't open the door, an' the window's not locked. So he's out a hour at least, an' it'll only take ten minutes for me an' the Nabber to get in an' out."

"I was hopin'," said the Nabber, "he would of pulled yer inside, an' we could have all gone home an' never seen yer again."

The rest of the Cats had had similar hopes, though not as drastic as the Nabber's.

"If yer frightened, yer can stay in the alley wid Suzie," said Rocky contemptuously.

"Come wid yer," said the Nabber. "Anything's better than that!"

"Right den. Billy, you keep dowse across the road from the front door, an' hoot like a owl if yer see anythin' suspicious – like a scuffer or der Ratman. Beady an' Little Chan, you stay in the alley, an' if *youse* see anythin' suspicious, one of yer run an' tell Billy an' den—"

"He'll hoot like a owl," said the Nabber sarcastically, but Rocky ignored him.

158

"An' Beady, keep an eye on Suzie, an' *you* behave yerself, tatty-'ead – yer shurrup an' yer stay put, got it?"

Suzie, clutching a half brick, jumped up and down enthusiastically. "Got it!" she shouted.

"Shurrup, Suzie! Keep quiet, and don't throw nothin'. Right. Come on, den."

Quietly and apprehensively, the Cats took up their places. Rocky and the Nabber went towards the front door of the Ratman's house, trying to look innocent and natural – and inconspicuous, which they didn't manage. In fact, they looked furtive and suspicious, but fortunately there was nobody around to see them just then, apart from Billy who, sitting across the road on his tricycle, felt very conspicuous.

At the window they stopped, trying to look as though they were just passing the time of day – or night – while Rocky whispered, "I'll go in first. Keep dowse for me."

"Who's keepin' dowse for me, but?" the Nabber muttered.

"Billy is." Rocky slid the window up, and the smell of the house came out to him, but no sound. It was dark and still and silent in there, and it gave him a creepy feeling up his spine having to go in again. The window sill was quite low, so he didn't need bunking up. He crawled inside, switched on the torch and dropped down as quietly as a cat.

"Right, Nabber," he whispered. "Close the window after yerself."

159

In the darkness, the Nabber muttered, "Yer could have just dumped the parcel inside the window."

"This way." Rocky went into the kitchen, where the rats squeaked and ran away from the torchlight.

The Nabber muttered desperately, "This place is a sewer – come on, get out!"

"Not yet. I'm dumping the parcel here, among the boxes. He'll never notice it."

"Great. Can we go *now*?"

"There's the money ter get. Come on, along this passage – keep in the middle – things is piled up."

"Shine the torch round – can't see nothin'."

Cautiously Rocky opened the door into the room that had the desk in it. The torchlight flickered over the room and the Nabber breathed hard behind him as he looked over his shoulder.

Then abruptly, Rocky switched the torch off.

"What's it?" whispered the Nabber.

"He's here – in the chair. Asleep."

"Terrah well. . ."

"No – wait." Rocky switched the torch on again, cautiously directing the beam to the armchair, keeping it low. The Ratman sat there, upright, his face white and still as the moon, his arms lying along the arms of the chair and his bony hands drooping over the edges. His eyes were closed, and he was quite still. He didn't even seem to be breathing.

"He's had it," the Nabber hissed, but Rocky thought he was just asleep.

"The loot's in here," he whispered, and slid the drawer of the desk open. "Got the bag?"

They had just time to see that the drawer was empty except for one five-pound note when the Ratman got slowly to his feet, staring at them. He stretched out his hands to them and muttered, "There's light and. . ." before falling back into his chair.

Rocky heard the Nabber ploughing over the books and papers in the passage. He stayed a minute, shining the torch on the Ratman's face – his eyes were closed again – then he followed the Nabber.

As Rocky scrambled out of the window, he heard Billy hoot like an owl, and turning round quickly he had a glimpse of the Nabber running, when he was grabbed from behind, an arm tight across his chest and a voice said, "Right – wur's the smack?"

Rocky squirmed desperately. "Haven't got. . ."

Something pricked against his neck.

"This is a knife, wack," said the voice, and the man's breath was on his face. "Wur's the smack?"

"S'in der," gasped Rocky. "In der kitchen. .." This was true.

"I'll just start with a small nick, then I'll. . ."

"It's true – tellin' yer, mister. Go an' see – yer welcome to it. . ."

Where's the Cats, he was wondering desperately, when he heard Beady shout something, and saw the Cats coming towards him, shouting all together. He heard Suzie shout something she shouldn't have, and he saw her raise her hand to throw the half brick.

It must have hit his attacker right in the back, because he gasped and loosened his hold. Rocky kicked him hard on the shin, and twisting round

161

butted him in the stomach with his head. Then he yelled, "Out!" and the Cats raced off along the alley towards St Catherine's, Billy pedalling fast, Suzie yelling, "Out! Out!" and the Nabber well ahead.

A voice behind them shouted, "Dan'll get yer for this!"

They stopped in St Catherine's Square, breathless, anxious and not inclined to hang about.

"Feel as if I'd been through a car wash," said Beady.

"Is he comin' after us?" asked Little Chan.

"Don't think so," said Billy. "Would have been here now."

"Unless Suzie's brick did a serious injury," said Beady. "Who was he, anyway? Just came out of nowhere. . ."

"Be Murky Evans," said the Nabber. "His gang'll be after us now − dey use razors. An' der's a zombie in that house, an' we got nothin', an' what with the zombie an' Murky Evans after us, we might as well go an' be garden gnomes in the Wirral!"

"Wasn't Murky Evans. He's not out yet − I checked," said Beady.

"Yer didn't take nothin' then?" asked Billy, relieved.

"Der was a drawer full of money − I saw it − he took the fiver out of it, but it's been done. Somebody's been in. An' that was one of Dan's gang got me − he was only interested in the heroin. Was goin' ter cut me up. . ."

"What did you do with the heroin?" asked Little Chan.

"Put it in der kitchen wid der boxes. Just wonder about the Ratman. Think he could be dead."

"Got on his hindlegs, didn't he?" asked the Nabber. "Well, thanks very much. It's been great. First der was the gold an' silver, then there was the heroin, then there was the drawer full of money. S'been interestin', even if we didn't get nothin' out of it except the Crown Street Gang on to us an' a bunch of pushers from Joseph Terrace. An' there goes Halley's Comet," he added, as Suzie revived and started racing round the Square, shouting, "Out! Out!"

"S'all happenin' here."

At that moment Mrs Flanagan shot out of the door of Number 3 and demanded to know what they were all hanging about round there for, and didn't they have homes to go to, and "Get yerselves in, Rocky and Suzie."

The Square emptied as fast as a can of Coke on a hot day. Reluctantly Rocky and Suzie followed Mrs Flanagan into Number 3, but as they went along the passage there was a shouting from upstairs and Ellen-from-upstairs's husband, in his best suit and carrying a suitcase, came down the stairs, pushing them out of his way and departing through the front door without a word. At the same time, Ellen-from-upstairs's head appeared leaning over the banisters, her long blonde hair falling over her tear-stained face, as she shouted, "Don't leave me! Come back, John!"

163

Mrs Flanagan shouted indignantly, "Wur's yer manners, you?" But he had gone.

They all looked up, shocked, at Ellen, who wailed, "Oh, Mrs Flanagan! What'm I goin' to do?"

"Yer'll get yerself and Trevor down here, an' yer'll have a cuppa an' a talk. Get yerself inside, Suzie, or I'll batter yer. Wur've you two been, anyway? An' put the kettle on, Rocky." And she sailed into the flat like the QE2 on its way to New York, dignified and organised.

Rocky filled the kettle and put it on without any enthusiasm. He felt tired and very worried.

"He's left us," Ellen was sobbing, sitting opposite Mrs Flanagan in front of the electric fire. "He's left me an' Trevor – and he said he loved Trevor an' he would never leave us! And he *has!*"

"It's men. Yer can't trust them. Look at Flanagan," suggested Mrs Flanagan. "I'll be lucky if I ever see *him* again, either! There's some bacon der, Rocky. You could make some butties. What's the matter wid this feller John?" she asked Ellen.

"Says I'm a slut! A slut! An' Mrs Flanagan, I've wore meself out lookin' after him an' ironin' his shirts an'—"

"What about them butties, Rocky?" demanded Mrs Flanagan.

"Don't want a butty," said Rocky, handing round mugs of tea.

"Yer don't want. . .?" Mrs Flanagan was struck dumb for a moment. "What's wrong wid yer?"

"Not hungry."

164

"Not. . .? Don't believe it. Der must be a blue moon. Here, Suzie, have a look through the window an' see if der's a blue moon!"

Puzzled, Suzie went to lift a corner of the curtain and peer out. She turned back, looking worried. "No moon," she said to Mrs Flanagan.

"What's dat?" Mrs Flanagan was engrossed with Ellen.

"No moon."

"Gerraway, yer daft thing! There's one good thing in this," Mrs Flanagan went on judicially. "When it comes ter the divorce, he can't get Trevor."

"Don't think he'd want to," said Ellen.

"Well, yer well rid of him. . ."

Suzie, angry and frightened, went over to Rocky. "No moon, Rocky," she said. "No moon."

"Yes, der is, tatty-'ead, but it's not out yet, see? It'll come round later. Here's yer butty. Get yerself sat down wid it."

He felt sick and couldn't face a bacon butty, which was a wasted opportunity, but it wasn't until he went to bed, lying awake in the darkness, that fear overcame him.

The Nabber was right, really. It *had* been a disaster, and Dan would send somebody else after him. And the Ratman would find the money gone, and tell the scuffers it was him and Nabber Neville who had taken it. He could see clearly in his mind the Ratman getting up and staring and then sitting down, and he could feel the cold and hear the rats. He could be ill, the Ratman, or dead. The rats could start eating him, once they had

165

got through the pies and heroin. But who *had* taken the money? Was nobody could get into that place until he'd unlatched the window, and he was the only one, apart from the Cats, who knew about it. What could he do? Who could he tell about it all? Flanagan wasn't back, and the wingy wouldn't forgive him for breaking into the house.

But he had to do something about the Ratman. . .

"Wonder if he's dead, the Ratman."

The Cats did not reply immediately to Rocky's comment. They had avoided the subjects of the Ratman and Dan all day, because they didn't want to consider them, and they were going home along Princes Boulevard instead of Larkspur Lane because they didn't want to meet up with any of Dan's mob.

"We can't just let him die there by himself," said Rocky. "Could go back inter that house again ternight. Find out if he's dead. Yer'll come wid me, Nabber?"

But the Nabber shook his head and his hat. "No way I'm goin' back inter that house," he said.

Rocky felt the same. But he *had* to do something. "I'll have a word wid der wingy," he decided. "He was a friend of der Ratman. He'll do somethin'."

"He'll have a word with McMahon," said Beady.

"That's right," said the Nabber. "Then we'll all be taken in on suspicion. An' they'll search the house and find the smack. . . But maybe this feller Dan's mob'll get us before then and save the scuffers the bother. . ."

"We must stay at home at night," said Little Chan.

166

"Yer can't spend the rest of yer life stayin' home at night!" exclaimed the Nabber derisively.

"Yes, he can. It's a free country," said Beady.

"Free? Yer have ter be jokin'," said the Nabber. "My dad says this country is a tax trap. *He* says he's givin' it up, an' we'll go ter Australia!"

The Cats were astounded by this as they contemplated the possibility of losing the Nabber to Australia. Then Rocky said, "Well, yer'll have ter get a different hat, won't yer? One wid corks hangin' on it!"

"Corks!" exclaimed Beady. "What's he want corks on his hat for?"

"To keep the flies off. Yer shake the hat, see, and the corks—" Billy began, but the Nabber interrupted,

"Have ter give it to him. He hasn't got a holler head like some people. Could put him in a quiz show."

"Course yer could. Told yer was a good skin, Billy. An' listen," Rocky added, as Howard skated up to them, "I don't want ter hear nothin' about trouble!"

"Wasn't goin' ter say nothin' about trouble," replied Howard, aggrieved. "Was goin' ter say about the match."

"Haven't had time ter think about that," said Rocky, which was true.

"That's good, because we're takin' in the bets in handfuls!"

That didn't help, because the Cats knew which team it was that the bets were going on.

"Dey're bettin' wrong, den!" shouted Rocky. "We'll show youse!"

Howard skated round in a circle, thoughtfully. "Can always try," he concluded at last. "There's trouble—"

"Told yer not ter say that!" retorted Rocky.

"Over there. . ." and he skated away.

And there was trouble. Ahead of them they could see through the grey dusk and drizzle the flashing lights in front of the Ratman's house.

"He's got the scuffers in about the missin' money," said Beady.

"No." Rocky sounded thoughtful. "He wuddent – got too much ter keep quiet about."

"They're on ter the drugs then," said Billy.

"Cuddent be. . ."

As they got closer to the house, they could see an ambulance and a police car down Crown Street, and a policeman on the Boulevard keeping the traffic moving, a crowd being kept back and all the lights on in the Ratman's house. They stood inconspicuously on the edges of the crowd, and saw two men in the two front rooms moving about there and in the kitchen. Then a man who was carrying a doctor's bag came out, got into a car and drove away, and two ambulance men carried out a long plastic bag on a stretcher. There was somebody in the bag.

"He *is* dead," muttered Rocky. "The Ratman."

Rocky had to talk to somebody about the Ratman, so he risked meeting up with Mrs Oliver and rang the bell at Mrs Abercrombie's. It was the wingy, however, who opened the door.

"Mr Oliver – yer heard about. . ."

168

The wingy was looking very sad. "I have, Rocky," he said. "Been over there and had a word with Mac. Mac found him. Saw a window was open and went in. He was sittin' in his chair, dead."

Must have been dying when me and the Nabber were there, Rocky thought. Must have been. So they couldn't have done anything about it. They could of been the last people he saw. He felt sorry for the Ratman, dying alone in that house.

"What he die of?"

"They don't know yet. Could be natural causes – could be the cold. Mac says the place was like a fridge, and full of rats. Could have been a robbery and the thieves killed him. There was suspicious circumstances – the window open. . ."

"Anything missin'?"

"They don't know – don't know what was in the place. But one or two small things could have gone, because there's spaces in the dust where things had been, and they think there must have been cash about, but they couldn't find any."

Rocky wanted to know whether they'd found the heroin, but he couldn't ask about that. Anyway, he thought, it would take them a lot of time to find anything in that mess.

"I blame meself, yer know, Rocky," went on Mr Oliver.

"What for but? Yer thought he was dead long since."

"Well, I used ter know him, didn't I? An' *you* told me about the house, an' I should have gone over, made some inquiries, done somethin'. . ."

"Yer cuddent have done anythin', Mr Oliver," said Rocky, and he meant it. What could he have done for the nutter when he was dealing in heroin? It would be a shock to the wingy if he ever found out about that. It would be a shock to him if he ever found out that Rocky had been involved with the Ratman.

Then he suddenly realised that Mr Oliver would never know he'd been involved with the Ratman. The Ratman was dead, and Dan wouldn't be bothering him – he would shut up shop when he knew the Ratman was dead. Rocky was in the clear!

"Hi, Mr Oliver," he said, "yer cuddent have done nothin', so stop blamin' yerself."

"Well, life has ter go on," said the wingy, but he didn't seem any more cheerful. "And on top of everything, it's me birthday."

"Well, go and have a pint, Mr Oliver," Rocky urged. "Have a chat wid yer mates."

"That's a nice thought, Rocky, but I'm out of funds. The wife's sequestered them."

"Here, Mr Oliver, have this." He gave him one of Joey's five-pound notes. "Have this one on me."

"Couldn't do that, Rocky," said Mr Oliver firmly. "And anyway," he added suspiciously, "wur'd it come from?"

"Our Joey. Done a job. Give us all money. Go on, Mr Oliver. Yer've done as much for me."

"Well thanks very much, Rocky. Yer a good skin. And thank your Joey when he's back, and congratulate him on his success. Never thought he'd make it. What's he in to?"

Rocky side-stepped that question. "We've got a match fixed wid de Allsorts, an' I think we'll get some tiddlers from Joseph's for supporters."

"But they've never supported the Cats' team!"

"Think they've been converted." At ten pence each, he added to himself.

"How many tiddlers we got?" asked Rocky.

"Ten," said Billy, frowning down at his notebook. "An' they know they don't get paid if they don't behave themselves."

"Right. Over here, all on youse!" Rocky shouted. The Cats' team left off warming up, and the tiddlers joined them, as did Suzie, though she started jumping up and down and drawing attention to herself.

"Now listen. Youse lot from Joseph's – yer on *our* side, see? Yer cheer when we score, and yer shout for us all der time. Yer shout, 'Come on the Cats' and 'Dey are de champions', an' yer can shout at the Allsorts when they come on, 'Their wingers is all tortoises!' an' anything else yer can think of. And mind, der's money in the game."

"Wur's it, but?" asked the tiddlers' leader.

"Yer'll get it when yer've deserved it. An' listen, Cats, the backs'll have ter watch the goal – they've got a good striker. An' Nabber, stick ter Howard like a limpet, an' Beady, if yer can get the ball ter me or Little Chan, do it, an' we'll do the rest. An' ignore the noises off."

"We come for the money," put in the tiddlers' leader, "but we come as well because yer a friend of Dan's,

171

right? An' Mickey says to ask yer if yer've got any smack, because he's gettin' desperate, an' he can pay – he's just sold a trannie."

"Listen, you," said Rocky, angry, "I'm not a friend of Dan's and I haven't got any. . ."

Just then the Allsorts came through the gates, and he had to concentrate on the game, though sometimes he couldn't help thinking of Dan – and Mickey.

It was a good game, and they kept the wingy busy, and it was mainly because the Cats were feeling that they had nothing to worry about so far as the Ratman and Dan were concerned. It was all over. So they scored first, but then Howard tackled Little Chan, got the ball and took it up to the Cats' goal, where the goalkeeper messed it up and did an own-goal, and the tiddlers couldn't be heard over the noise from the Allsorts, even with Suzie's help. Nothing much happened after that until just before time Beady got the ball to the Nabber who sent it to Rocky (and then fell on his face), Rocky got it to Little Chan, who scored, and the wingy blew the whistle.

"Here, wack," said Howard, coming over to Rocky. "You cost me a lot there."

"Should only back winners."

"Be different next time!"

"Believe it when it happens! Youse all did well!" Rocky told his team. "We'll not put any of youse on the market!"

"Best you've done yet, Cats," said the wingy. "But the Allsorts are good – could have been an off day for them. Don't forget that."

"Was all due ter me," said the Nabber. "If I hadn't got the ball. . ."

"Rocky, got somethin' ter tell yer." It was Billy, who had freed himself from the tiddlers, having paid over the money to their leader and watched for a worried moment as he disappeared under them.

"What's it, skin?" asked Rocky, his red hair standing up in spikes from the towelling he'd been giving it and his eyes fierce with triumph. "What's it?"

"Not good, Rocky. Think they're jacks."

The two men who had got out of a car at the park gates and then stood watching the game were obviously plain-clothes, as Billy had suspected. And they were still watching – watching Rocky.

Pretending not to be worried, Rocky pulled on his sweater, thinking fast.

"Billy, can yer get the Cats' team to do a diversion? The whole lot going together out through the gate – tell the Nabber he's leader, because I'm limping. An' can yer see that Suzie's all right?"

"Do me best. Nabber'll be easiest. Get him ter organise it. What yer think they're after, Rocky? Think they've found the heroin? Think Dan's been. . .?"

"Don't know, skin. Listen. I'll gerroff. Get the team organised, an' I'll contact yer somehow. An' thanks, wack!"

As the Allsorts and the Cats streamed out of the gate into Princes Boulevard, Rocky ran for some bushes, pushed through them and came face to face with the old man in the raincoat and black scarf and black woolly hat who'd been eating sandwiches beside the lake. He took one look at Rocky and started off in the other direction, his right hand clutching his left wrist, where his watch was.

"Sa'll right, mister," Rocky panted. "Wasn't goin' ter. . ."

But there was no time to explain, and he shot out of another gate into Ullett Road and then took a long way round back to St Catherine's Square.

But as he went into Number 3, he saw a car stop beside Mrs Abercrombie's. It was the same car – same men – jacks!

CHAPTER
11

He couldn't get into the flat. His mother was out, and the door locked. Knowing the police would come to Number 3, he ran upstairs and knocked on Ellen-from-upstairs's door. She opened it slowly, Trevor in her arms, and smiled at him. She seemed a lot happier.

"'Lo der, Rocky," she said. "How's things?"

"Can I come in, Ellen?" asked Rocky desperately.

"Course yer can. Come on."

As she closed the door behind him, Rocky felt safer. The scuffers wouldn't look for him in Ellen's.

"Sit down, Rocky. Like somethin'? Got some Coke."

"Thanks very much. I'm that thirsty I could drink out of a sweaty boot."

Rocky relaxed while Ellen got the Coke. He thought she had a nice place. "Yer've got a nice place, Ellen," he said, drinking some Coke and feeling better. "The furniture. . ."

"Me husband bought it. He was all right to begin with, yer know like, Rocky."

"An' dat picture. Dem boats all still on der sea – dat's nice."

"Was a weddin' present from his auntie. He left it.

Think it's near Blackpool. Think it could be worth a lot."

They both heard the car outside, and Ellen went to look out of the window. "Hi, Rocky," she said. "There's two fellers comin'. . ."

Rocky leapt up to see. It was the jacks.

"Dey're lookin' for me. . ."

"What yer done, but?"

"Nothin'. Haven't done nothin'! But listen, Ellen, can I hide somewhere – if dey come up here?"

"But, Rocky. . ." Ellen looked at him, worried. Then she said, "All right, then. Seein' it's you." She looked round the room, thinking desperately, then said, "Under the bed. In here."

It was dusty under the bed.

He heard them knocking on the door, and Ellen opening it.

"Rocky? He doesn't live here – it's downstairs. . . Well, his mam must be out, then. . . No idea, she could be back any time, yer know like. . . All right, then, I'll tell her. What's it about, but?"

At that point Trevor crawled into the bedroom and paused to look at Rocky under the bed. He started making attempts at communication. Rocky didn't respond, but that did not put Trevor off – he started squealing. Rocky did a Doomlord face at him, but he only squealed louder, and Rocky was relieved to see Ellen's legs and feet.

"S'all right, Rocky," she said. "They've gone. What they want yer for, but?"

176

Rocky crawled out. "Don't know. Haven't done nothin'. Thanks, Ellen. Do you a good turn when yer need it. Sure dey've gone?"

Ellen went to the window to check. "They're just drivin' away. But listen, Rocky, if yer in trouble, I don't want to be mixed up in it. Yer know like, I have ter think of Trevor."

Rocky went to sit on the stairs till his mother came back, but he was too worried to stay still, and went out to see if Mr Oliver was about. He was, but he was standing at the gate of Mrs Abercrombie's house, in serious conversation with Constable McMahon, so Rocky did a quiet U-turn and went back to sit on the stairs. He was very worried.

After a bit, Ellen-from-upstairs came down, carrying Trevor.

"Yer still here, Rocky?" she asked. "Yer mam not back?"

"Don't know where she's got to."

"Yer can go an' sit in my place if yer want," she offered generously.

"S'all right. She'll not be long now."

And a few minutes later Suzie dashed into the passageway, and stopped in astonishment when she saw Rocky on the stairs. She approached him slowly.

"Locked out."

"Dat's right."

Suzie sat down beside him and put her hand on his arm. "Sad, Rocky? Not happy?"

"Listen, Suzie, yer know what a secret is?"

177

Suzie looked at him and shook her head.

"Somethin' yer don't tell nobody about, see."

Suzie thought about it, then nodded. "Not tell."

"Right." But Rocky still had doubts about whether he could trust Suzie not to give him away.

"Wur've yer been, anyway, tatty-'ead?" he asked. "Yer look as if yer'd had a mud bath. Me mam'll go crazed."

Suzie took this very seriously. "Come wid you," she decided.

"Yer can't. Listen. I'm goin' ter live in der hideout for a few days."

"Come wid yer."

"Told yer, tatty-'ead, yer can't. An' yer tell *nobody*. Got it?"

Suzie nodded, still watching him seriously.

"Der'll be times, Suzie, when yer'll have ter get food an' things from Billy and bring them ter me in der hideout. Yer understand? An' yer don't tell nobody about it."

Dazed by the impact of all this information, Suzie nodded again, and Rocky wondered if she could do it.

"Yer know the secret knock?"

Suzie tapped it out on the stairs.

"Yer know ter go past, and just come in when nobody's around?"

Suzie nodded again.

"All right den. Now, what yer do if somebody says, 'Wur's Rocky?'?"

Suzie frowned fiercely, shook her head and said, "Gone."

178

"Gone wur?"

"Don't know."

"Comin' back when?"

"Don't know."

"Think yer've got it, Suzie."

Mrs Flanagan returned in a jubilant mood, carrying parcels. "Well, look at you two pudden-'eads!" she exclaimed, seeing Suzie and Rocky sitting on the stairs in the light of the low-wattage bulb. "What you sittin' there for?"

"Yer locked der door, didn't yer? We cuddent get in," retorted Rocky indignantly.

For once Mrs Flanagan was contrite. "I'm sorry, luv. I forgot. Here, come on in. Flanagan's comin', an' he's sent some money. Come an' see what I've got. . ."

Mrs Flanagan had got quite a lot. She'd got a new pair of jeans and a cardigan for Suzie, a new sweater and anorak for Rocky. An Oriental cooked chicken from Marks & Spencer's, a pack of frozen chips, a chocolate gâteau – Black Forest – and some cans of lager; as well as, for herself, two pairs of shoes, a new dress and three pairs of earrings, all from 'Coats and 'ats'. Having spread them around the room, she collapsed in her chair, kicked off her shoes and said,

"Rocky, luv, can yer make a cuppa? I'm as dry as a hot oven. An' can yer put dem chips in?"

Rocky went about things thoughtfully. He wanted a meal, but he also had to get away. Suzie, stunned by the jeans and cardigan and worried about Rocky going, fetched and carried plates and mugs.

179

"When'll he be back, den, Flanagan?" Rocky asked.

"Two weeks. Smashin', in't it?"

"Better let Joey know."

"I will. Soon as he comes. We'll have a smashin' party, an' we'll go down ter the Lanny and see his ship comin' in. It's all goin' ter be all right!"

Rocky could only hope that it would be – for him as well.

After they had eaten, Mrs Flanagan went upstairs to spread the good news to Ellen. Once she had gone, Rocky sat down and wrote:

> Dear Billy Suzie will bring this its all secret dont say nothin but yer can tell the Cats. The scuffers is after me so Im goin inter hidin she noes were. Its about the Ratman. Tell the Nabber to keep his head down and nobody comes to the hidout only you and Suzie and dont put yer bike near the place see nobodys watching. If anybody asks yer dont no where I am. Heres 3 pounds to get some food for me – plenty tea an conny in the hidout an I have plenty for 2 days after that bread butter corned beef anything like that. Destruct this. Thanks Billy yer a good skin. Rocky.

Suzie stood beside him, watching very seriously as he folded the letter and put it into one of his mother's supply of envelopes with the three pounds, sealed it, wrote 'Billy' on it and gave it to her.

"Put it in yer pocket," he said. "Yer know wur Billy lives in St Catherine's?"

Suzie nodded.

"Yer only give this ter him. An', tatty-'ead, be careful round der – don't go speakin' ter anybody an' come straight back. Promise."

Suzie promised. She never spoke to anybody but Rocky anyway.

Then Rocky scribbled a note to his mother on another piece of paper:

Dear mam, dont wory. Wont be around for a bit. Hav to go into hiding. Back soon. Dont tell anibody. Rocky.

He left it on the table, made a couple of sandwiches with some of the Oriental chicken, and a jam butty, and wrapped up some of the gâteau – his mother would never notice it had gone. He put it all in a plastic bag. Then he went into his bedroom and folded up the blanket, leaving the sheets in a rumpled state so that she wouldn't miss the blanket. Then he fished out of the cupboard the long bag with the shoulder strap his father had always taken with him on his voyages, and always brought back stuffed with presents.

He put the blanket and the supplies into the bag and slung it over his shoulder. It was dark outside now. He went to the front window and peered out. The Square was empty.

"Right, tatty-'ead?"

In the light coming from the street lamp, Suzie nodded.

Outside, he said, "Yer'll be careful, Suzie? Yer'll see Billy an' come straight back and yer'll talk ter nobody."

181

Suzie was used to looking after herself in the city, having run off so often. She grinned up at him, held up the letter and in the other hand a half brick. She's the ultimate weapon, Rocky thought, as he watched her race away, the tattered bow of ribbon in her hair waving behind her.

Mrs Flanagan came back from Ellen's, saying, as she pushed open the door, "Here, Rocky, have yer heard? Der's been a murder. . ." She stopped, and asked, "Wur's he?"

Suzie, sitting in front of the television, didn't even look round. "Bed," she said.

"He's early for once." Mrs Flanagan yawned. "Could do with a early night meself." She sat down in her chair, absently watching television, but looking thoughtful and a bit worried. Then she looked at Suzie and became even more thoughtful. Things would have to be all right when Flanagan came back, she decided. No good going on about Suzie to him – he might just take off with her. After all, she told herself, just look at what had happened upstairs. Still, Suzie wasn't one for saying much, but it would be best to. . .

"Suzie," she said.

Suzie only nodded, her eyes on the screen. She was watching a complicated murder mystery. Couldn't be taking it in, Mrs Flanagan thought, but you could never tell. She had never been able to fathom Suzie.

"Termorrer morning yer can try the jeans and cardie on – the jeans might have ter be shortened a bit."

182

Suzie looked round at her, surprised but also suspicious.

"An' yer dad's comin' back, so we'll have ter get him a little present, won't us?" Mrs Flanagan pressed on.

The word 'dad' only filled Suzie with a feeling of rejection and loss, and she suddenly stood up, fierce and frowning.

"No dad, no dad," she started.

Hastily Mrs Flanagan changed her tactics. "All right den, we'll have a chicken butty each – all right? An' I'll have a lager and you can have a Coke, all right?"

Suzie never refused any offer of that kind. She nodded and sat down again.

"Funny," muttered Mrs Flanagan, cutting up the chicken, "looks as if somebody's been at this. . ."

And in his bedroom, Billy was reading Rocky's letter yet again, and frowning over it. He'd passed the word round the Cats, and everybody was assuming a low profile. The Nabber had even persuaded his mother that he should go and stay with his uncle and aunt in St Helens for a couple of days. As he destructed the letter, Billy wondered whether Rocky was doing the right thing. After all, if the police weren't already looking for him, they certainly would be, once his mother reported him missing.

It took two nights for Rocky to go off the hideout. It was all right for meetings of the gang and playing cards and drinking tea and planning things, but it wasn't a place to live in – not in cold weather and by yourself. He kept the heater going, but it didn't make much impression on the temperature, and when he closed the shutters at night and lit the candles, the dimness was very depressing.

It took Mrs Flanagan the same length of time to discover that Rocky was missing. She had so much to do, what with the shopping and the bingo, deciding how to get the flat cleaned up before Flanagan's return, consulting with Ellen-from-upstairs and discussing things with Joey, who had come back, still wealthy and jovial but deciding to be away before Flanagan returned.

It was Joey who, after the second night of Rocky's disappearance, coming out of the bedroom in his pyjamas and looking for bacon and eggs, asked, "Hi, mam, wur's our kid? He didn't come in last night. Gettin' ter be a dirty old stop-out, in't he?"

Mrs Flanagan turned round from the cooker in astonishment. "Didn't come in? What yer mean, didn't come in? *She* said he'd gone ter bed," and she pointed a fork at Suzie, who was sitting on the bed, her back to the wall, glaring at both of them.

"Well, *she* never knows what's up, does she? He could of come in and went again. But *I* never saw him." Then he added, "Think he could of. . ."

"Run off?" Mrs Flanagan asked. "What for but? He's gorra good home here! He wuddent do that!" Then she sat down. "He's been murdered! Here, Joey, get yerself down to Larkspur Lane an' report it. Go on, while I get myself ready. . ."

But going into a police station was the last thing on Joey's agenda. "S'all right, mam. He'll be back. Could be stayin' wid one of his mates. Nobody would want

184

ter murder *him*, anyway. Forget it, an' let's have me nosh."

"Yer can finish cooking it yerself," said Mrs Flanagan, putting on her coat with a fierce look at Suzie who, she suspected, was behind it all.

"Look, mam," said Joey complainingly from the cooker, "there's no need for der scuffers ter come inter it. He'll be back. Yer'll see."

"If Flanagan comes back an' that lad's missin', it'll be bonfire night. Clear up when yer've finished, and *you*," to Suzie, "get yerself dressed."

As the door slammed behind her, Suzie disappeared under the bedclothes and Joey, yawning, took his plate of bacon and eggs to the table and, while eating them, considered what his next move should be.

The police station in Larkspur Lane was a single-storey building in red brick, which had an ecclesiastical look because of its pointed arch windows, and inside it did have the look of a run-down Sunday school. It also had a notice board outside, on which were pinned notices with photographs or identikit pictures of people wanted or missing, and warnings to the public of various legal or illegal things they could get up to. But even this was not safe from the graffiti artists, because there was a small but accurately drawn portrait of the police sergeant just down beside the pavement, with 'Wanted' printed underneath it. The same sergeant, at his desk at the end of the entrance passage, looked up from his reports when Mrs Flanagan presented herself desperately before him.

"Now then, Mrs Flanagan," he asked, "what's to do?"

"It's Rocky. He's gone. Run off. Hasn't been home two nights."

The sergeant's attitude changed, but almost imperceptibly, to one of serious interest.

"Run off? Why didn't you report it sooner?"

"Just discovered it. See, Suzie said he was in bed, an'. . ." Mrs Flanagan burst into tears. "Yer've got ter find him before he's murdered! I love that lad's *bones!*" she sobbed.

"Now, this isn't goin' ter help, Mrs Flanagan. It doesn't sound serious yet, but yer'll have ter give us the details. Here, come through and have a cuppa, and I'll get a message out to the cars. . ."

The Cats' special knock wakened Rocky from a doze, and he cautiously opened the door. Billy and Suzie came in quickly, and Rocky bolted the door behind them.

"All right, skin?" he asked.

"No, Rocky. It's not." Billy was frowning anxiously. "I brought these things," he said, putting a plastic carrier on the table, "but I don't think yer'll need them."

"What yer mean? What's happened?"

"Yer mam's been ter the police about yer, and they've started a search. They're going through everythin'. They'll come here – bound to."

Rocky couldn't understand it. After all, he'd left his mother that note.

"What'll yer do, Rocky?" asked Billy.

186

"Better clear out."

"Where to, but?"

Rocky couldn't think of anywhere. "Dey been askin' questions, the scuffers?"

"Asked Little Chan an' Beady an' me – about that house, and where you might have gone to, and where we last saw you."

"Anybody clatted?"

Billy shook his head. "Nabber hasn't been questioned. He's back, but his mam says he's not well. What *will* yer do, Rocky?"

The two anxious faces looked at Rocky in the candlelight. And he didn't know what to do. Just then they heard footsteps on the steps down to the basement, and voices. Rocky blew out the candles, and they listened in the darkness, with Suzie holding on to Rocky's anorak, as somebody pushed at the door.

"Locked. Sure this is a possibility?" It was McMahon.

"He's been hanging around here." It was Mr Oliver's voice. "But I don't think he'll be in there – not unless he's been in and took ill."

"Need somebody's permission to break in. Leave it just now. . ."

The footsteps retreated.

They stayed silent and tense in the darkness until there were no more sounds from outside, then Rocky hissed, "He's clatted on me, the wingy – ter the scuffers!"

"Could just be wantin' ter find yer, make sure yer safe," whispered Billy. "Don't think the wingy would clat on yer – yer know he wouldn't."

"Yer can't trust nobody."

"Can trust me."

"Yer right. I can. Have ter get away before they come back."

"Where'll you go to, but?"

"Don't know."

"Yer should maybe talk ter the scuffers, Rocky. Would maybe be best."

"Not talkin' ter *them*. Will yer go out, Billy, an' have a look round der Square – see it's clear, an' I'll make a run for it."

"But, Rocky—"

"Go wid yer." Suzie's voice came out of the darkness.

"Yer go wid Billy, tatty-'ead. He'll get yer home all right. An' I won't forget yer help, wack. Go on. . ." He struck a match and cautiously opened the door: some daylight came into the hideout. It was quiet outside. Billy went up a couple of steps and peered through the railings into the Square. Apart from Beady's mother and a neighbour gossiping and looking in the other direction, there was nobody about.

"S'all clear," he whispered.

"See yer then!" and Rocky leapt up the steps.

He leapt right into Constable McMahon, who had cunningly been waiting out of sight round the corner.

Rocky squirmed and twisted, and yelled, "Geroff, scuffer! I'll do yer! I haven't done nothin'! Geroff!"

"Yer not gettin' away, so yer might as well give it up."

Then Mr Oliver said, "Come on, Rocky. Give it up. It'll get yer nowhere. . ."

188

Rocky stopped struggling to glare at him, his eyes tiger-fierce, his red hair bristling. "Yer clatted on me, didn't yer? Yer did! *An'* yer owed me!"

"Got it all wrong, Rocky. Was for yer own good. Ter help yer!"

"If that's helpin', what's yer idea of harmin'?"

CHAPTER
12

It was surprising how quickly a crowd could collect –
Beady's mother and her neighbour, the woman from
Number 4 and Mr Oliver's wife, and Ellen-from-
upstairs with Trevor.

"What yer doin' to him?" Ellen asked indignantly.
"What yer doin'? He's been lost. He should have a cup
of tea!"

"He'll get one," said McMahon grimly. "Now come
on, Rocky."

"It's what's ter be expected from that lot," said the
woman from Number 4.

"Shurrup, you! You can talk!" retorted Ellen.

"Yer right. I can. I know about you an' yer goin's on
– *and* his mother's as well!"

"What yer mean, goin's on? What yer mean?"

"That's enough," said McMahon. "The show's over.
Anybody know where Mrs Flanagan is?"

"She went out lookin' for the boy," said Beady's
mother. "Joey went as well. I'll keep a look out for
her."

"I'll come with yer, Mac," said the wingy.

"Yer'll not. Don't want yer around," said Rocky.
"Ellen, will yer look after Suzie till me mam's back?"

190

"Course I will, luv. An' I'll tell yer mam. But I think dis is disgraceful. Come on, Suzie."

"Not go," said Suzie, and came out with a word she shouldn't have, to give her opinion of the constable.

"Yer have ter go, Suzie. An' behave yerself. Billy, yer'll see ter things?"

Billy nodded, and Rocky walked away with the constable, asking, "Wur's der handcuffs, but? I'm a dangerous criminal, in't I?"

The desk sergeant welcomed him. "Ah, Rocky! So yer've been found."

"Was never lost." Rocky glared at him. "An' I want ter know why dey brought me in, an' I want a lawyer."

"Why not have a cuppa first and a bit of a chat?"

He sounded so kind and persuasive that Rocky looked at him suspiciously, and began to wonder whether he'd been wrong and they'd only brought him in to ask where he'd been and how he was. He relaxed a bit. At the back of his mind he recalled that this was the second time in his life he'd been brought in, and both times he'd been innocent – well, nearly innocent. That confirmed his belief that the scuffers, whatever you did for them, would always pin something on you if they could get away with it.

"What yer want ter chat about?" he asked contemptuously. "I don't generally chat wid scuffers."

"Well, Rocky, that makes me sad," said the sergeant, "but maybe yer'd make an exception this time? Now if yer'll just go with Constable McMahon. . ."

The constable's hand fell on his shoulder, and Rocky twisted away. "Geroff! It's disgustin'! Geroff! Yer not takin' me. . ."

But he was taken, quite swiftly, into the detention room and sat down on a hard chair behind a plastic table. A WPC came in with a mug of tea.

"There y'are. I put two sugars in," she said soothingly.

"Well, yer can drink it den! When's the chat start?"

The WPC sat down on a chair in a corner and got out her notebook. Rocky recognised the signs, and he didn't like them. "I want ter know what. . ."

At that moment, he heard his mother's voice raised in anger, in the corridor. "Wur is he? Wur *is* he? I'll batter him for this! I'll belt him round. . ."

Soothing noises from the sergeant, then, "Calm down? Calm down? After all I've been through? Wur did yer find him? Wur *is* he? An' I don't need ter be led around – get yer hand off or I'll marmalise yer!"

Rocky looked up as his mother's face appeared in the pane of glass in the door, and he put his face in his hands.

"Now, me lad, I want an explanation. Wur yer been? What yer been doin'? Der's Flanagan coming back, and wur'll *you* be? In jail! Yer know what a time I've had? Yer got any idea? Me hair's turnin' white – look at it – in't it?" she demanded of the WPC, who only offered a mug of tea.

Rocky pushed his mug over to his mother. "Can have dis one. I'm not havin' it. An' I left yer a note," he said quietly.

192

"Yer left a what?"

"Don't get airyated. Dey take down everything yer say!"

Mrs Flanagan got the message. She sat up straight and glared at the constable. "I'll have a private word wid my son," she said, and to Rocky's surprise she got it. McMahon and the WPC went out, though McMahon still observed them through the glass.

"Now what's happenin'?"

"I left a note for yer, on der table, tellin' yer not ter worry but I had to go inter hidin' fer a bit. Did you not see it?"

Mrs Flanagan was suddenly thunderstruck. "That? Thought it was a spare piece of paper – wrote me shoppin' list on it. Look, it'll be here. . ." and she started scrabbling in her handbag.

"Doesn't matter. Just ter let yer know I didn't just walk out."

Mrs Flanagan was penitent. "I'm sorry, luv. I reelly am. Yer see, I was in such a state, an'. . ." She thought for a moment. "What yer have ter go inter hidin' for but? What yer done?"

"I haven't done nothin'."

"Well, we'll have a lawyer. We're entitled ter one. Dey can't just keep yer here. . ."

She prepared to go and bone the sergeant about it, but was stopped by the entrance of two men in plain-clothes, whom Rocky recognised.

I've had it, he thought desperately. It's not about me – it's about the Ratman.

In the corridor, the wingy was consulting with the sergeant.

"How's it goin'?" he asked.

The sergeant was no longer genial.

"Two of the detectives on the case are talking to him. I think it could be serious, Dave. I think he might have ter be taken to Cheapside."

"Ter the Bridewell? Yer can't mean it! Rocky couldn't have done anything ter justify that. I know he gets up to things he shouldn't, but not. . ."

"We'll have ter see, Dave. It looks as though there's drugs, robbery and maybe murder involved."

"Yer jokin'! Yer daft! He's not that kind of lad! Can I do anything? His step-dad's still away, and his mother can't cope with this kind of thing. Trouble is, Rocky's gone off me. Thinks I shopped him. Which I didn't. Wouldn't have, whatever he'd been up to."

"Hope you would, if drugs was involved. Anyway, I'll try and have a word with him – clear yer name for yer, right?"

"Clear Rocky's name first. More important. And I can't see yer've got anythin' on him."

The sergeant did not respond to this, and the wingy went to sit on a chair against the wall, rested his chin in his one hand and looked gloomily at the opposite wall.

"Now, that house on Crown Street – you know the one I mean, and what happened there?" It was the senior jack talking. Had to be the senior one, because he was fatter, Rocky concluded.

"What house in Crown Street? What yer on about?" demanded Mrs Flanagan.

"The one they found the dead man in," Rocky explained.

"That one? What's that got ter do with us?"

"I think Rocky knows what I'm talking about. He had some interest in that house. . ."

"That's daft. We never knew the feller there. . ."

"You were seen looking over the wall there, and you talked to Mr Oliver about the things inside."

"But he's never *been* inside!"

"Shurrup, mam. Yer not helpin'. Knew it was McMahon an' the wingy shopped me. Knew it. Listen, mister, yer know all *I* know about der place. Told McMahon about the feller we saw come over der wall – *he* could of got inside. An' I've seen the old man walking round at nights – give me an' Suzie a fright. Was a nutter, yer know like. But dat's all!" he concluded, with more conviction than he felt.

The detectives exchanged looks, then the younger one asked, "Recognise this?"

'This' was a plastic bag with whitish powder inside that Rocky did recognise. It was now sealed inside another plastic bag. Rocky was sweating. He didn't look at the detectives. He prepared to put on his innocent air.

"This evidence, is it?"

"Could be."

"What's it, but?"

"Think you know."

195

"Bit daft, yer mate, in't he?" Rocky asked the other detective. "Know what it could be. Flour, is it? This the big baking mystery?" He wasn't feeling as cheeky as he sounded.

"It's heroin. Are you a user?"

"Him? A user? You mind yer lip! I'll have Flanagan on ter yer! We're a respectable family! I'll get the law on ter yer! An' anyway," Mrs Flanagan added, as extra proof of Rocky's innocence, "wur'd he get the money from for it?"

"Got any money, Rocky?" asked the older one. Rocky could feel a web closing over him, a sticky web.

He shook his head.

The detective sighed. "Let's see what yer've got in your pockets."

Sullenly Rocky deposited on the table two biros, one used bus ticket, a notebook, some loose change and his membership card for the Baptist Youth Club. He did not produce the twenty-five pounds.

"That all?" The older jack sighed. "Turn the pockets of your jeans inside-out, and let's have your ano-rak."

Rocky protested, but it was no good. The younger detective went to work on his anorak, while the other one examined the pockets of his jeans, so it was the older one who put the bundle of notes on to the table and carefully counted them.

"Twenty-five pounds," he said.

"Can count, then!" retorted Rocky.

"Where did it come from?"

196

"Yer can stop yer flamin' suspicious questions!" burst out Mrs Flanagan. "Was his brother Joey give him thirty pounds, and he give me sixty, and he give our Suzie five, because he's got a good job."

Rocky sank back in his chair, appalled. She's shopped our Joey now, he thought, for he didn't believe Joey got that money honestly.

That gave the detectives something to think about. Rocky could see their brains working.

"Joey has a record, hasn't he?"

"He was framed – an' it's no thanks ter you lot he got himself a proper job!" retorted Mrs Flanagan.

"Where's he working?"

"Well – I'm not sure. . ."

"We'll need to have a word with him."

"Whenever yer like."

"Where is he?"

Mrs Flanagan hesitated. "Don't know. But he'll be back soon."

The jacks had gone silent, and were occupying themselves with something else, which was worrying. They were looking over the notes and a notebook, a notebook with black covers. It was like the one that Rocky had seen on the Ratman's desk. The senior jack looked up.

"Mrs Flanagan," he said, very seriously, "we have a list, made by the old man who lived in the Crown Street house, of the numbers of the notes kept in a drawer in his desk. The numbers on two of these notes that Rocky has tally with some of those in this notebook. But you say Joey gave Rocky the notes?"

197

Mrs Flanagan did not take in the implications of this. "Told yer," she said. "Our Joey's got a job. . ."

"Have you any of the notes Joey gave *you*?"

"Course not – I bought things. . ."

"Where is Joey, Mrs Flanagan?"

Rocky sank back in his chair. It was Joey and his pal who had done the Ratman's house – that had been the job he'd been on about, and they must have got in through the window he'd left open and they could have killed the Ratman. But Rocky couldn't see that happening.

"We don't know where Joey is," he said.

"Does Joey use heroin, Mrs Flanagan?"

"I've told yer – we're a respectable family!"

"Doesn't always mean anything when it comes to drugs." He thought for a few moments, then he said, "We'll have to question Joey, Mrs Flanagan."

As his mother protested Joey's innocence, Rocky got hold of his anorak and the contents of his pockets, including the loose change, but as his hand reached out towards the twenty-five pounds, the younger jack stopped him.

"Have to leave that, Rocky. And we'll want statements about it. And about this."

He pushed another plastic envelope across to Rocky. Inside, it had a sheet of white paper, and on the paper was typed, 'Ask Rocky O'Rourke about the smack in the Crown Street house.'

"What about it?"

Rocky knew immediately. It was Dan who had sent that, typed on his expensive notepaper, Dan getting his

198

own back. Dan fixing him. He didn't look up at the two jacks, and he didn't say anything.

Suzie was sitting on the stairs at Number 3 when a car stopped outside. Before the front door was pushed open, she was hiding in the space under the stairs where the dustbins were kept. She peered out and listened to voices upstairs, and then ran.

Ellen-from-upstairs opened the door when the bell rang, and was confronted by a stranger. She had already heard a taxi draw up outside and the doors slammed, and here was a man she didn't know, tanned and with a case and a packed bag slung over his shoulder. He had a relaxed, outgoing attitude that rather worried her.

"Hello, dur," she said, clutching Trevor.

"I'm looking for Mrs Flanagan. Me wife. Can't get an answer down there."

Ellen flinched. What could she say?

"Yer Mr Flanagan? Well, they'll be that happy. . ."

"Wur are dey, but?"

Stunned, Ellen said, "Well – is Mrs Flanagan not in?"

"Told yer she wasn't."

"Well, Suzie – is she not on the stairs?"

"What would she be on the stairs for?"

"Well, she was with me, but then she said she would sit on the stairs till her mam come back."

"She's not there."

Ellen shook her long hair back from her face and said, "Oh, I hope she hasn't run off again."

Mr Flanagan dropped the bag from his shoulder. "Look," he said, "I just want ter know where the family is. What yer mean Suzie's run off? Wur's me wife, and wur's Rocky?"

Ellen hesitated, making up her mind, then she said, "Don't know wur Suzie is. But yer wife an' Rocky's at the police station in Larkspur Lane. Yer could go down there, but if yer'd like a cup of tea first. . ."

"What they there for?"

"Well, I don't really know, but there's some trouble. I don't know, but I think it's with Rocky."

Mr Flanagan thought for a moment. "Can I leave me luggage wid yer?"

Ellen smiled. "Course yer can. Oh, an' listen. Yer could have a word wid Mr Oliver. He's the caretaker at Mrs Aber's on the corner. Yer should have a word. . ."

CHAPTER

13

"Jim Flanagan!" Mr Oliver got up as Flanagan came into the police station. "Yer back! Thank God for that!" He held out his hand.

"What's goin' on, Dave? The girl upstairs says me wife and Rocky's down here and Suzie's missin'. What's it all about?"

"Ah," said the sergeant, "yer must be Rocky's step-dad?"

"That's right. And I want ter see him *and* me wife, and I want to know—"

"Just a second," and the sergeant went off to the interview room.

"Can't get the hang of this, Dave. What a home-coming!"

"Well, yer come at the right time. It looks serious. They think Rocky's got into drug-dealin' an' burglary, maybe even. . . well, they'll tell yer."

"That's rubbish!" exclaimed Flanagan. "Unless he's changed out of all recognition – rubbish! He's no angel, but—"

"Flanagan!" Mrs Flanagan, followed by the sergeant, the two detectives, the policewoman and Rocky, came out of the interview room and flung herself at her husband, sobbing, "Yer wuddent believe what's happenin'! Yer cuddent! Dey'll jail him – Rocky! Jail him!"

Flanagan put his arm round her. "Stop janglin' on, woman, will yer? Now then, son," he said to Rocky, "what yer been up to?"

Rocky glared at him. "Nothin'. Not been up ter nothin'. What *you* been up to?"

"Now listen, lad, you mind yer lip! I'll sort *you* out sharp! An' where's Suzie?"

Mrs Flanagan dried her eyes. "With Ellen-from-upstairs."

"She's not. Ellen says she's run off—"

"No! She cuddent of! I can't take all this – not on top of everythin'!" cried Mrs Flanagan. "An' it's not *my* fault! She's *your* daughter!"

"Mr Flanagan," said the sergeant, trying to impose some order on the Flanagan family's chaos, "if I could just explain about—"

"Look," (Flanagan was getting upset) "I come back home an' me daughter's missin', me wife's in hysterics, Rocky's goin' ter jail and we have a grand reunion in the local lock-up!" And he started an argument with the detectives, the sergeant and McMahon.

"Listen, Rocky," said Mr Oliver, "I didn't clat on yer. Yer know I wuddent. Yer can't think. . ."

But Rocky wasn't listening. He took advantage of the turmoil and departed, running.

The Cats were outside, in a huddle.

"What's happenin', Rocky?" asked the Nabber.

"They lettin' yer go?" asked Billy.

202

"Have youse seen Suzie?" asked Rocky.

They hadn't.

"Don't tell the scuffers which way I went! See yer!" And Rocky started for the Steps. He had to find Suzie. He could guess what had happened. She had seen her dad and didn't want to know him any more, and she didn't know where Rocky was, so she had nobody and she'd run off. That took his mind off his own problems – he could sort them out later.

Suzie wasn't in Number 3, and she wasn't in the builder's hut or the abandoned car or the launderette.

"Me sister been in?" he asked the woman in charge. "Yer know – she come an' sat here. . ."

"She's not been back. Is she lost?"

Rocky stopped to think. Where would she have gone? Must be somewhere she felt safe in – somewhere she knew. He ran back to the hideout, but she wasn't there. Then he had an idea.

As he ran along the alleys towards Crown Street, he heard the sirens of a fire engine on the Boulevard and smelt smoke. Then he stopped as he saw a drifting cloud of smoke in the sky ahead, with red flames in it, and heard shouting in the distance. There was a bang, and over towards Lodge Lane the sky was suddenly on fire. Rocky started running again.

As he turned into Crown Street, Howard skated past him.

"Bad news, lah!" he shouted. "Bad trouble! Upper Parley's burnin'! Lodge Lane's a battlefield!"

203

The crowds in front of the Ratman's house were being held back by police as they watched the firemen dousing the blazing roof of the Princes Gate Hotel with water.

"Like the Blitz, in't it?" an old man said in a nostalgic voice.

Rocky pushed through the crowd, using fists and elbows and feet. At the front, the smoke was choking, and it was hot from the flames. He was making for the hotel when a policeman seized him by his anorak.

"Get back!" he ordered.

"But – me sister – she's. . . she could be in der!"

"Nobody's in there."

"Yer don't know – I have ter . . . Hi! look at dat!"

As the policeman turned to look, Rocky pulled himself free, ran and leapt over the low wall in front of the hotel, sprayed by water and shouted at by firemen. He pulled a handkerchief out of his pocket, put it over his nose and mouth, ducked his head, pulled his anorak over it and stumbled into dense smoke. He dropped to the floor and started crawling through the room where the tea chest was that Suzie had got into. He had to make sure she wasn't there now. He couldn't see, but he groped round till he found it, and put his hands inside. Suzie *was* there, but she didn't move or speak. He heaved her out and started dragging her towards the door. He could feel the heat from the floor even through the thick soles of his mukluks. Then he collapsed, choking with the smoke.

★

It was only when he woke up that the smell of burning and the crackling of flames left him, but the soreness when he breathed and the smarting of his eyes were still there. He was in bed – a strange bed, but it was very comfortable. It was in a long room with a lot of other beds, kids in some of them, kids wandering round, kids with bandages and clutching soft toys.

Suzie, he thought suddenly, remembering the burning hotel and Suzie in the tea chest, and he sat up.

"Wur's Suzie?" he shouted. "Did yer get her out?"

Some of the kids gathered at the bottom of the bed to look at him.

"Will yer clear off?" he demanded. "Hi, who's in charge here? I want ter know. . ."

A nurse came to him. "How do you feel?" she asked.

That wasn't important. "Wur's Suzie?" he demanded. "Did they get her out?"

"If you mean the little girl you were brought in with, *you* got her out."

"An' she's all right?"

"She will be."

"Wur's she?" He got out of bed.

Suzie was in a small room at the end of the ward. She was very pale and sound asleep.

"She *is* all right," said the nurse.

"Doesn't look like it. Was she burnt?"

"No – just the smoke. . ."

Rocky took hold of the hand that lay on the blanket. "Suzie," he said. "Yer all right, Suzie?"

Suzie stirred and opened her eyes.

205

"Yer rubbish!" Rocky exclaimed. "What yer do it for, Suzie? Yer could of ended up like a packet of crisps!"

"You swine," said Suzie, and closed her eyes again.

"Yes," the nurse commented, "*she'll* be all right."

"I'll geroff den," said Rocky.

"No, you won't. You'll get back into bed, Rocky."

"How d'yer know me name?" asked Rocky suspiciously.

"There was a membership card for the Baptist Youth Club in the pocket of your jeans. It had your name and address on. We contacted the police, and they told your parents and they came in. They'll come and collect you and your sister as soon as the doctor says you can leave."

"Yer told the – the police?"

"Of course. And they told your parents. Now, into bed. You'll have your lunch soon."

Never should have joined that club, Rocky decided, sitting in bed and wondering what to do next. Got nothing out of it, but they got his address, and the scuffers were told he was here. Balefully he watched the nurses going up and down in their smart white outfits.

Then he remembered the sky red with flames and the crashing and shouting and the Princes Gate Hotel burning. Had been right, had Howard. The trouble had come.

They brought him mince, mashed potato and carrots, and apple tart and custard for lunch. Great, he thought, as he got through it. Not bad places, these hospitals. I'll come again. Then, his mind going

206

back to his personal troubles, he asked the nurse who was taking his empty plates away, "Hi, missus. Any scuffers round here?" He spoke confidentially.

"Scuffers?"

"Fuzz. Police."

"Were you expecting them?"

"No." Rocky was all innocence. "Just wondered like. If yer had criminals in and. . . Listen, missus, if me mam an' dad come for Suzie, yer'd better watch it, because she'll either start screaming or she'll get under the blankets. An' yer'll never get her out."

"What are you talking about, Rocky? What do you mean?"

"Mean she hates me mam, and she hates her father because he left her with me mam, see? So yer'd better watch it."

She just smiled at him and said it was time he had another sleep.

They think I'm an idiot, he thought, but I'm not. And I'm not lying here waiting for the scuffers to come and get me.

"Hi, missus," he shouted to a passing nurse. "Wur's me things?"

"You mean your clothes? They'll be in your locker, by the bed."

Rocky got up, got his clothes out of the locker and headed for the nearest bathroom, where he got dressed. Then, when the coast was clear, he discharged himself from hospital.

★

Just round the corner from the hospital was Upper Parliament Street, and it was a disaster after the riots. Whole buildings gone and firemen still damping down fires, their hoses snaking over the debris-filled road. But there was a baker's shop and an Indian take-away doing business from behind shattered windows. Rocky was tempted by the take-away but he thought a hamburger and a can of Coke from the baker's would be more useful. Then he went to the shop next door, and got a BMX magazine and the latest copy of the *Eagle*. He paid for everything – he didn't want trouble. Then he got on a bus that took him along Princes Boulevard, and from the upper desk he saw the street down to St Catherine's Square, and the Ratman's house. Its roof had fallen in, and its windows were broken, and the Princes Gate Hotel was a total write-off.

Then he moved quickly back from the window. At the gate of the Ratman's house the wingy was deep in conversation with a man in overalls who was unloading something into a skip in the front garden. That was a near one. The wingy was sharp: one glimpse of Rocky and he would be down to the scuffers. Made yer sick, thought Rocky, scowling. After all he'd done for the wingy – and he'd scatted on him. He not only felt in danger from the thought of being up in court and put away for carrying drugs and taking money he never took, but he also felt he was without any friends. The Cats couldn't help him: they wouldn't want to get involved. Anyway, he couldn't see the Chans, or Billy's parents, or the Nabber's or Beady's mother saying, "Come on in – we'll hide yer

208

from the scuffers." No way. The only possibility was Flanagan. He'd been all right, had Flanagan – but could he be trusted now?

Rocky got off the bus at Princes Park and went through the ornamental gates and along the broad, pot-holed gravel path that ran alongside the place where the Cats had played football. It was deserted under a grey sky, and a cold, gusty wind was whipping at the trees. A park worker, fat and scowling, drove a wagon filled with branches from trees past him and a few minutes later came back with the same load, stopped and lit a cigarette. There was a hut, lit up and looking warm, with some park workers inside, drinking tea and play-ing cards. Not bad, that, Rocky thought. If he got out of this mess, maybe he'd get a job like that, sitting in there playing cards when it was cold and the only other work was sitting on a machine trundling rubbish around or cutting grass. Was an idea.

He wondered what they were paid, and went on to the shelter by the half-empty lake. Wouldn't be a duck for anything, he thought, wedging himself on the bench in a corner of the shelter where the wind wouldn't reach him, and tucking his feet up to keep them warm.

He unwrapped the burger and started on it, glaring ferociously out at the world. I'm innocent, he thought angrily. Innocent – didn't take nothing!

It was getting too dark to read his comic and too cold to hang around much longer. He dropped the empty Coke tin and the hamburger paper, pulled up the hood of his anorak and pushed his hands into the opposite sleeves. He could move soon, and nobody would notice his red hair. He'd have to go home. Just wished he could trust Flanagan to believe him.

The sound of footsteps approaching and a squeaking noise made him freeze. He saw silhouetted against the grey water of the lake a familiar group – someone on a tricycle, someone in a cowboy hat and two others.

"I'm goin' off this," said the Nabber's voice. "He's probably got on a boat and cleared off like Joey did."

"Got ter find him, Nabber," said Beady.

"What for but? He got himself inter the mess – like he always does."

"He is a friend," said Little Chan earnestly.

"He's trouble. We're givin' dis up. If he's as clever as he thinks he is, he can look after himself."

Rocky sat still, but he was furious with the Nabber.

Then Billy said, "I think Rocky's over there – in the shelter."

"Yer right, wack!" Rocky exclaimed, going over to them. "And thanks, Nabber – yer a real mate, you are!"

"It's him – cod's head!" exclaimed the Nabber, pretending delight.

"Give yer chin a rest, Nabber," retorted Rocky. "Youse lot been follered by the scuffers?"

"No. We looked out for dem all the time," said Beady. "An' Mr Oliver said we had ter look everywhere ter find yer."

"He said dat? I'm off! De scuffers'll be here any minit! He clatted on me, did Oliver. . ."

210

"He didn't, Rocky," said Billy. "Honest. He told us. An' he got McMahon ter tell us. And McMahon said yer should come back – der'll be no trouble, but there's information dey need. . ."

"An' yer mam's in permanent hysterics," said Beady.

"An' dey're after your Joey, because of the money," said the Nabber.

"Dat's me mam's fault," said Rocky unhappily. "But she didn't mean ter. . ."

"Family of unsuccessful criminals and nutters you lot are," said the Nabber.

"I'll spit in yer eye an' blind yer!" shouted Rocky.

"An' I'll purra lip on yer!"

After that they both calmed down, having enjoyed the exchange of compliments.

"Right," said Rocky. "I can trust der wingy?"

"Sure of it, Rocky," said Billy.

"He's never clatted – yer know dat," said Beady.

"Right," said Rocky. "I'll go an' see him."

There was a light showing through the fanlight above the door of Mrs Aber's house, but no sign of the wingy. Rocky risked ringing the bell. After a bit the door opened, and the wingy was there, surrounded by an aroma of fried liver and onions.

"Rocky," he said, and came out, closing the door partly behind him. "Yer all right, Rocky? Did the Cats find yer? Did dey tell yer. . .?"

"Dey did, Mr Oliver." Rocky was shivering with cold. "An' I'm sorry I doubted yer. But I was in a state and – what's goin' ter happen now? I'm just

211

hangin' around hidin' from der scuffers. Can't keep on wid it."

"Der's no problem, Rocky," said the wingy. "Well, der's not much of one."

"How d'yer mean like? I'm desperate!"

"The old feller – they've had a look at him, an' dey think he was bitten by a rat and got tetanus. Not certain yet, but it looks like it."

Rocky leant against the wall in relief. That cleared him. The Ratman couldn't scat on him, and he hadn't been murdered. He thought of him, getting out of his chair and looking at him and the Nabber and then sitting down. Could have been dying then. For a minute, he was sorry for the Ratman dying alone in that cold, dirty house. Then he thought, well, he *did* blackmail me, and he *was* into drugs.

"All right then," he said, "so they've got nothin' on me now, de scuffers?"

"Yer know, Rocky," said the wingy, going off at a tangent, "I was talkin' ter the feller that's been cleanin' that house out. Said when he started sweeping down the cobwebs, they covered him like a blanket, and he was shovelling dirt six inches deep from the floors. Filled four skips with books and old newspapers and food. Wish I'd known about it. Could maybe have helped him."

"Listen, Mr Oliver, yer shouldn't waste yer time on him," Rocky burst out. "He was a drug dealer and a blackmailer—"

"Yer know about that?" The wingy sounded surprised, though he wasn't really. "Well, yer could maybe help them down at the station with their inquiries."

Rocky backed off. The wingy *was* going to clat on him.

But Mr Oliver went on. "Yer should know, Rocky, that a young kid threw himself off the top of Joseph Buildings this morning. They think he was on drugs and his supply had been cut off."

Rocky said nothing, but he knew it must have been Mickey, and he remembered him pleading for smack and scratching at Dan's window and looking like a cave insect. He suddenly felt furious about the Ratman and Dan and the drugs, and he made up his mind – he would clat for the first time in his life!

He pulled the small change he had out of his pocket. "Can yer lend me a ten-pence piece, Mr Oliver? Only got fives, an' I have ter make a phone call."

"Good idea, Rocky. An' are they givin' yer a medal?"

"What for?"

"Savin' Suzie."

"Had ter save her, Mr Oliver."

He went into the phone box on Larkspur Lane. He could just about find the number of the police station in the directory by the light from the newsagent's. He put his handkerchief over the receiver and dialled. He recognised the sergeant's voice straight away.

"It's about the old man an' the drugs," he said in the gruffest voice he could manage. "Got it solved yet?"

The sergeant said they were working on it, and could they have his name.

"Some information for yer," Rocky went on. "Yer should make some inquiries at a grocer's shop back of the Cathedral, an' yer should have a word with Dan at 23 Joseph Buildings."

There was a pause then the sergeant said, "Thanks, Rocky. Hope yer feelin' better."

Rocky slammed the receiver down. Scuffers! he thought. Know everything!

Outside Number 3 St Catherine's Square, Ellen-from-upstairs was lifting Trevor out of the pram. "Oh, Rocky!" she said, thunderstruck, when she saw him.

"'Lo der, Ellen." Rocky was subdued, cold and not knowing what he was going to have to face.

"Rocky – I'm proud of yer. Yer that brave!" Ellen gave a sob and went upstairs. "Yer mam an' Flanagan's in," she shouted over her shoulder.

Rocky went into Number 3. His mother and Flanagan were sitting on either side of the electric fire, and looked round. Then Mrs Flanagan shot out of her chair and threw her arms round him, shouting, "Rocky! Yer've come back! An' yer a good lad – savin' Suzie!"

"Wur's she?"

"We've got her back – she's in bed. They couldn't find yer in the hospital – wur've you been. We've been that worried. . ."

Rocky waited for Flanagan to show his hand. Eventually he said, "I'm grateful to yer, Rocky."

"Think nothin' of it."

None of them knew what to do next, so Mrs Flanagan said, "I'll put der kettle on. Yer hungry, Rocky? We've got chicken for termorrow, and there's sausage an' eggs an' bacon an' pizzas an'. . ."

As she went on with her inventory, Flanagan said, "I'm sorry, Rocky, takin' so long ter get back."

"Up ter you, in't it?"

"Have ter get things cleared up with Larkspur Lane."

"Cleared it wid them."

"Yer have?"

"Never done nothin', yer know like. Never took nothin'. . ."

"But Joey did."

"That's Joey's business."

"Yer right. . . Here, I've got some things I brought back. Haven't had time ter think about them." He pulled a bag from under the table and started to unzip it. "Can't remember what's in this. . ."

He started pulling things out: a Japanese doll, two bottles of perfume, a roll of purple silk, a large bottle of whisky, a Chinese jacket and trousers (small size), a ship in a bottle, one Australian hat, a picture of a sunset, an African mask, a Chinese dressing-gown with gold and silver dragons all over it, small size, another ditto, large size. They were spread all over the table, and Mrs Flanagan gazed at them, ecstatic.

"S'fantastic! Don't believe it!"

Rocky personally thought it looked like an expensive jumble sale.

"What's it, Rocky?" asked Flanagan. "Nothin' I've brought back right?"

"Well – der hat. . ." Rocky tried it on. It might outclass the Nabber.

Mrs Flanagan, in a Chinese dressing-gown, was dabbing perfume behind her ears in between watching the sausages cooking. "We'll put der things on der wall tomorrow," she said, "an' all we want now is Joey back."

"What yer really want, Rocky?" asked Flanagan.

"Yer really want ter know?"

Flanagan nodded.

"A few pounds ter buy me pals some fish an' chips, an' a BMX."

"Yer on." It was a fiver. "The bike'll come later."

Suddenly Suzie appeared, like an underweight ghost. "Rocky," she said.

"How's it, tatty-'ead? Yer comin' out for some chips?" asked Rocky.

Suzie just stared at him. Then she looked at Flanagan and started off – "You. . ."

Rocky grabbed her. "Look at all dis, tatty-'ead, what yer dad's brought yer. Yer remember yer dad?"

Suzie turned her attention to what was on the table, and later, wearing the Chinese dressing-gown and clutching the Japanese doll, she actually smiled at Flanagan, and when Mrs Flanagan served sausages, eggs, bacon and chips, Suzie smiled at her, before dropping the doll and starting to make a chip butty.

That night, reading the BMX magazine in bed, Rocky was thinking of the Ratman, living alone in that house with the rats, sitting up in his chair and looking at him and the Nabber, when he was dying. Maybe he didn't know what he was doing when he was selling the heroin. Or maybe he did. Just wanted more and more money.

"Tatty-'ead," he said, and Suzie sat up, still clutching the Japanese doll. "Learn yer ter swim termorrer. Got yer cozzie?"

They started off next morning, suitably dressed – Suzie in the Chinese jacket and trousers and a conical hat, and Rocky wearing the Australian one. They were both wearing their mukluks, and they did not go unnoticed along Princes Boulevard, though Rocky traded insults with insults, and threats where necessary. The only person who was absolutely struck dumb was Howard, who nearly fell over and had to grab a wall.

There weren't all that many people swimming, so Rocky let Suzie flap around in the shallow end while he did a bit of diving and underwater swimming. Then he got out and said to Suzie, "Come on then, tatty-'ead, we'll do a bit of travellin'."

Suzie climbed out. "What yer mean, Rocky?"

With Suzie on his back, Rocky shouted, "British Airways Flight 727 leaving for Paris!" ran along the side of the swimming pool, shouted, "Take off!" and leapt into the pool.

When they both came to the surface, Suzie was coughing and spluttering, but she said, "Again, Rocky!"

"Right. Where'll we go this time? New York?"

Suzie nodded frantically, but before they could start the woman pool attendant came over. "Give that up," she said. "You're running, shouting and bombing, and it's against the rules."

"Right, missus. Don't get in a twist about it," and Rocky and Suzie walked to the end of the pool.

"Not bombin'? Not goin' ter New York?" asked Suzie.

"Course we are. Get on me back," and a second later, Rocky was racing round the pool, shouting, "Pan-Am Flight 202 leaving for New York! Take off!"

"Take off!" yelled Suzie, and they both submerged and came up again, spluttering.

The bath attendant blew her whistle, and came to the edge of the pool. "I'll not warn yer again," she said. "Running, shouting and bombing. Now you settle down, or yer don't come in here again."

Rocky reflected. "Right, missus," he said, but considering that their time was up anyway, he said to Suzie, "Wur d'yer want to go next?"

Suzie, not having much geographical knowledge, said, "London."

And with her on his back, Rocky raced round the pool shouting, "BA shuttle flight for London. . . Take off!" and leapt into the pool.

The whistle blew as he came to the surface, but he ignored it, grabbed Suzie and hoisted her out. "Get yerself changed, and I'll see yer at der front," he said.

Damp but warm, they returned along the Boulevard towards the Baptist Church, because Rocky meant to settle the business of the Christmas party. The hall was a hive of activity, as usual, increased by a number of members at a long table, who were putting things into plastic carriers. Betty Malloney was filling up mugs of tea, but she missed a mug of tea entirely when she saw Suzie and Rocky, and a lot of the other activity ceased.

"'Lo der, Betty," said Rocky, being friendly. "Watch it wid der tea. Can me an' me sister have a cup?"

Betty glared at him. "She can't, but I suppose you can, if you've paid yer subs."

"Goin' ter pay them. I'll have a word wid that fellow with the granny glasses about Suzie. Hi, when's the Christmas party?"

Betty stopped pouring tea, and looked at him. "We're not havin' one this year. The committee decided we would spend the money on parcels for old people."

"I don't believe it! What yer think I pay me subs for? Where's de point in payin' me subs?" demanded Rocky.

"It is better to give than to receive," said Betty Malloney, virtuously.

"Wur's that feller Hunt?"

"He'll be in soon."

Rocky looked round in disgust. He would give it up, the youth club. It was all outgoings and no incomings. Then he contemplated the table, with the willing helpers filling plastic bags. He went over to see what was happening. Every bag had a small tin of corned beef, a small tin of tomatoes, a small tinned pie, two oranges, a small Christmas pudding and a Christmas card being put into it. After watching the proceedings for a while and choosing his time, Rocky picked up one of the plastic bags.

"Come on, Suzie!" he urged, and they went out together.

"Goin' ter Prinney Park – see if de old man's der," he shouted.

The old man was there, sitting on the bench, watching the ducks and eating a sandwich. He did not welcome Rocky's appearance. He shrank back, picked up his plastic bag and started to move, but Rocky was determined.

"Hi, mister! Not goin' ter mug yer. Got yer Christmas present. Here – s'not a bomb – s'groceries and dat sort of thing. An' if yer don't take it, I'll flatten yer!"

That persuaded the old man, and he took the bag and looked into it. Then he smiled at Rocky. "Thanks very much. Kind of yer."

"Think nothin' of it. Paid me subs for it, see. Was due ter me. Terrah well! Come on, Suzie! Yer've got yer mukluks on – yer can have yerself a paddle."

As they both walked cautiously into the mucky waters of the lake, Rocky was thinking that that afternoon he would get the Cats together and let the Nabber see his hat. But first he'd get Flanagan to hang some corks on it!

Mrs Flanagan had agreed that Rocky could have the Cats in for supper, since the place was cleaned

anyway. Rocky went off on his new red BMX –
better than Joey's bike – to the Indian take-away.
He tried one or two experiments with it on the
way, but two were unsuccessful and he ended up on
the pavement, so he didn't try any on the way back
with the carrier bag full of curry and chips slung on
the handlebar.

When he got home, Mrs Flanagan, slightly dazed,
was looking at a postcard that had arrived. Obviously
she had done nothing to prepare for the Cats' arrival,
which happened almost immediately, with the Nabber
shouting outside, "Hi, Rocky!"

"Oh, my God, they're not here!" cried Mrs Flanagan.
"And there's our Joey in Spain. Look, Rocky, he's sent
this, but we haven't got ter say nothin' ter nobody
about it."

"Wasn't goin' ter, but," said Rocky, and went to
let in the Cats.

They came in rather reluctantly, standing beside
the door and wondering what to do next. Then
Mrs Flanagan put Joey's postcard in her handbag,
put on her coat and, saying she was going to
find Flanagan, departed. After that, the atmosphere
was more relaxed. The Cats sat round the table,
the Nabber in his cowboy hat, Suzie in her Chinese outfit, while Rocky in his Australian hat and
mukluks put the plates out and shared out the
curry and chips. Suzie started to make a curry
and chip butty.

"That yer BMX outside?" asked the Nabber.

"That's right."

"Looks great," said Beady. "Can I have some more Coke?"

"*I'm* gettin' one," said the Nabber. "When me dad comes. Bigger than yours, but."

"Would be, wouldn't it," said Rocky. "Yer a bigger nit than me – need a bigger bike." They all laughed, ignoring the cobwebs over the cooker that Mrs Flanagan had missed.

"Joey's gone ter Spain," said Rocky.

"Could afford it with all that money," said Little Chan.

"If I hadn't left the Ratman's window open, Joey couldn't have paid his fare to Spain," said Rocky.

"They could extradite him, but," said Billy seriously.

"Would that be terminal?" asked the Nabber, and Beady choked over his curry.

"This is not bad," said the Nabber, sitting back in his chair. "An' I've got something important ter say." He paused, waiting for their attention.

"Gerron wid it well," said Rocky. "Youse'll have to go home soon."

"Well, I have ter hand it to you, wack. Yer did a good job, savin' *her*," pointing at Suzie, "even if *we* got nothin' out of all the rest."

Suzie dropped her butty and glared at him. "You swine!" she said.